REVENUE VS. SALES

WINNING IS A PLANNED EVENT

THE FOUR BOOK COMPILATION

By Mort Greenberg

First Paperback edition August 2025

Print Paperback ISBN: 978-1-961059-22-1
Kindle KPF ISBN: 978-1-961059-23-8
Ingram EPUB ISBN: 978-1-961059-24-5

Published by digitalCORE
www.dgtlcore.com

digitalCORE

Other Books by Mort Greenberg

REVENUE VS. SALES SERIES

- **The Singular Focus**
  100+ Tips to Maximize Your Revenue

- **Revenue Boost**
  The Ultimate Sales Plan in Five Steps

- **Straight Up Selling**
  Your Toolbox for Sales Excellence

- **People Drive Revenue**
  Talent Systems That Deliver Results

THE FOCUSED SELLER SERIES

- **Maximizing Human Performance in Sales**
  Unlocking Your Best Results By Thinking
  Like A Business Owner

- **The Sales Tactician**
  Spycraft Techniques for Revenue Success

- **Elevate**
  Mastering the Art of Sales Leadership

- **Beyond The Acquisition**
  Thriving With Private Equity Ownership

CHILDREN'S BOOK SERIES

The Fearless Girl and The Little Guy with Greatness

- **Book 1** - Live Life Motivated
- **Book 2** - Young Leaders Guide
- **Book 3** - Asking Awesome Questions
- **Book 4** - Think to Win
- **Book 5** - Smart Money Moves
- **Book 6** - Wellness Warriors
- **Book 7** - Travel Like a Pro
- **Book 8** - Outdoor Skills

THIS BOOK IS
DEDICATED TO THOSE I
SPENT THE MOST TIME
WITH AT REGENT LP'S
MEDIA BIZ KNOWN AS
ARCHETYPE. THROUGH
MANY BUSINESS
CHALLENGES, THIS
TEAM DELIVERED
FOR THE 8+ YEARS WE
WORKED TOGETHER.

KELLY FACER (GSD BOSS), **STEPHANIE GILDEA** (MARKETING DOER), **WILL "THE HOODIE KING" ALEXANDER** (RINGER OF REVENUE FROM ALL FOUR CORNERS OF THE SCREEN), **MATT GROSS** (SURE. GIVE ME A DAY), **SYDNEY BROWN** (NO PROB. WE CAN DO THAT), **MINDY MORGAN** (AD OPERATIONS), **AIDALINA MARTINEZ** (ANY REQUEST, ALWAYS PERFECTLY EXECUTED), **CHRISTINE ANDERSON** (KNOWS WHEN EVERY DEAL NEEDS TO GO LIVE), **MEGAN GIORDANO, MATT MILES AND CARLI PANTELIDIS** (ACCOUNT MANAGEMENT THAT IS ALWAYS ON POINT), **SHERRI FISHER** (SELLER TRUTH METER), **SHAVON DIXON** (CONSTANT POSITIVITY) **JAMIE ELLIOTT** (NEWSROOM WRANGLER), **HUGH GARVEY** (A STORYTELLING GENTLEMAN) **THOMAS STORY** (PHOTOG OF THE WEST) , **TRACY SENG** (TRULY UNIQUE PARTNERSHIPS), **PAMELA COFFEY** (THE ICONIC HEAD OF SUNSET TRAVEL SALES), **ROBERT SITCH** (DEFENSE BRAND GURU), **TED CHASE** (NEW BUSINESS KICKSTARTER) **PILAR ALLAS** (MILITARY SPECIALTY SELLER), **DRUCIE DEVRIES** (THE CUSTOMER'S CHAMPION), **DIANA SCOGNA** (INTERNATIONAL INTRIGUE), **LEWIS DUNCAN** (KING OF EMAIL PROSE), **CHRIS BRIDGHAM** (CAN YOU HEAR ME?), **LAUREN BABBAGE** (WE CAN MAKE A SHOW ABOUT THAT!), **TODD SOUTH, LEO SHANE III, JON SIMKINS, KAREN JOWERS, SEBASTIAN SPRENGER, BEN MURRAY** (KEEPING SERVICE MEMBERS AND THEIR FAMILIES IN THE KNOW), **AND, ROB WILKINS** (THE EVANGELIST). **PLUS "THE LA TEAM"** THE REAL MR, BOBBY HOERNSCHEMEYER, THOMAS WEHINGER, ADAM PUGACH, DIDIER DIELS, GRADY SHEINBERG, MIKE MARTIN, TOM GRIFFITHS, MARC MENARD, ANI ABRAHAMYAN, COLIN HIRSHLAND, NICK TERRY, SUNNY PARMAR, ANTHONY DEPATIE, VINCE JOVIN, RYAN FARBER, **YONG KORMAN,** MAURICIO COS, BRETT GAMBLE, FARRUKH AWAN, FABIAN SPEIGHTS AND APRIL DITTO

WHAT OTHERS ARE SAYING ABOUT THE AUTHOR

Kenny Wachtel I Formerly SVP of Sales for Excite@Home

One day back in 1997, Mort, who I had just promoted to Sales AE, approached me as the CRO at an early internet startup named Excite, and told me that we should buy a small company called eBay. They weren't on anybody's radar back then. This is the kind of guy that Mort is -- able to peer into the future and bring potential opportunities into the present. Due to the efforts of sales executives like Mort, Excite grew its valuation from $100 million to over $6.7 billion at merger 3 years later. A go-getter, closer extraordinaire, and future forecaster all wrapped in one package. I wish that I had more Morts on the staff.

Matt Gilbert I Former SVP IAC / InterActive Corp and current CEO of Partnerize.

When it comes to building a sales organization capable of sustained excellence, there is no better architect than Mort. Revenue Boost captures the key pillars upon which Mort enabled tens of millions of dollars in sales with the type of cost efficiency that makes CFO's smile. Over a 5-year period at Ask Jeeves, Mort's approach underpinned a turnaround effort that materially contributed to a valuation increase from $33M to an exit to IAC / InterActive Corp of $2B. Following the acquisition, Mort's playbook was the foundation for the creation of IAC Advertising Solutions, a business unit that was responsible for the monetization of all advertising inventory across a portfolio including Ask.com, Expedia, CitySearch, Ticketmaster, Evite, Match.com, Lending Tree and more.

Allen Blum I Former SVP Time Warner, VP NBCUniversal.

During Mort's time at NBCU, he was a key part of rebuilding the local television station group's push towards online and mobile platforms. Very often we would partner to create first & one-of-a-kind ways for brands to leverage both linear and digital to maximize their message and therefore attain their value propositions on a variety of geo-targeted platforms. Arguably, the NBC owned and operated station group covered the largest DMAs in the country and delivered 1+ billion dollars of revenue to the company's portfolio.

Kevin Dulsky |Formerly Nokia's Head of Global Mobile Advertising. Currently Partner Andreessen Horowitz

I was fortunate to have Mort as part of my leadership team. It was inspiring watching him run around the globe and motivate those on his team and win over clients new and old. He is an exceptional sales leader, and skilled communicator who can clearly articulate complex ideas. Mort's efforts and positive ways helped us navigate change in our division as Microsoft acquired Nokia's devices and services businesses.

Kevin Dorsey I Formerly President of National Media Groups, iHeartMedia. Now running his own media and digital advisory firm

Once Clear Channel obtained Department of Justice clearance for the acquisition of Westwood One's Metro Traffic division Mort ran the day-to-day process to integrate this unit with our wholly owned subsidiary Total Traffic Network and lead our sales team. The combination of two $100M+ businesses into one became Total Traffic + Weather Network.

Tim Horan I Chief Growth Officer, Pattern Health

Working directly with Mort I have seen first hand the consistent and predictable results his sales system delivers. Mort has always treated selling as a science, so if you are serious about elevating and optimizing you or your organization's performance, these are must read books for you.

Joe Britton I Founder & CEO SearchMarketers

Straight Up Selling is a MUST have for your entire sales team. So many books are too high level making it difficult to learn where to start or how to execute. Straight Up Selling provides you with clear and concise tools and tactical steps to crush your sales goals. Not only have I used this method when working in big corporations, but also applied these exact tools to build my company to the #4 Fastest Growing Company in America - Deloitte. There are MILLIONS of dollars worth of secrets to fast track your sales success in this book!

Jim Diaz I Former VP / SVP, Sales Excite, Ask Jeeves, Turn

Mort and our teams scaled multiple digital sales driven companies from millions to hundreds of millions of dollars in annual revenues over the course of a decade. He was instrumental in innovating the transformation from purely relationship driven, transactional selling to automated sales through platforms driven by real time analytics. Mort has an innate ability to thread the needle between humans and machines, creating sales strategies that sustain success over time.

Brian Berger I Founder and CEO Mack Weldon (Former Sales Colleague at Excite@Home)

Mort's straightforward and relatable style is relevant for

most sales situations. As colleagues, he always made our clients feel like was their advocate which was key in earning their trust. This was authentic and real – no BS.

Alex Boyce I COO / CBO Dash Radio/DXSH.MV

Mort was not only technically one of my first 'bosses,' but a friend, mentor and someone I credit with helping shape my career. Mort's focus on the difference between 'revenue' and 'sales' changed my perception of our objectives as sales leaders and was critical in my professional progression.

Jonathan Sandak I Founder WooHooMarketing and Account Executive, NBCUniversal

Mort focuses on helping sellers achieve their best. Four times over the years I have been on teams with Mort: IAC, Nokia, iHeartMedia, and Sunset Magazine. At each company we relied on the same systems in this book to plan our go to market strategy and scale our revenue. This book is as close as you can get to working with him 50+ hours per week.

Douglas Neiman I Founder & CEO Navio Networks

Mort is not only an experienced seller, but has always been an amazing listener to what clients need. He then leverages these two skills, coupled with incredible organizational talents, to create a system that continues to prove successful for all sellers who have worked for him.

INTRODUCTION

Revenue vs. Sales: Winning is a Planned Event

Revenue is the ultimate scoreboard. It is what every salesperson, every manager, every company, and every investor or shareholder is striving to generate. But behind every dollar of revenue is something even more important – a disciplined, consistent, and focused sales process.

Revenue vs. Sales: Winning is a Planned Event was created to help you build that process and sharpen your "Revenue Mindset." Whether you are just starting your career in sales, leading a team, running a business, or investing in one, this series will arm you with the practical tools and no-nonsense strategies needed to drive growth. Sales alone does not guarantee revenue. Only a structured, repeatable system – combined with relentless focus – does.

Inside this series, you'll find four books that bring to life the core of how I have run my teams, revenue efforts and process for planning any part of a business:

- **Book #1: The Singular Focus – 100+ Tips to Maximize Your Revenue**

  A fast, no-fluff 30-page handbook filled with practical lessons, hard-won experiences, and quick-hit advice. Divided into four key sections, it delivers the kind of insights you only learn through battle-tested selling, failure, and the wisdom of great mentors. Designed to sharpen your focus and eliminate distractions, this book will help you lock onto your goals like never before.

- **Book #2: Revenue Boost – The Ultimate Sales Plan in Five Steps**

  Success starts with a plan. This 80+ page workbook

walks you through a simple, five-step system to define your objectives, goals, strategies, measures, and tactics – all captured on a single page by the end of the process. With access to a companion 5-tab Google Sheet and Excel Workbook, you'll finish this book with a fully customized strategic sales plan that you can immediately put into action.

- **Book #3: Straight Up Selling – Your Toolbox for Sales Excellence**

   This is your no-excuses, straight-talking sales training manual. Across 150+ pages, you'll dive deep into 12 critical areas of sales technique and management that separate average sellers from elite performers. Plus, you'll gain access to 35+ downloadable Excel worksheets to reinforce your skills, track progress, and turn best practices into daily habits.

- **Book #4 - People Drive Revenue - Talent Systems That Deliver Results.**

   This additional Ten Chapter book inside of Revenue vs. Sales provides a tactical blueprint for building, managing, and scaling a high-performance sales team.

Revenue vs. Sales is built for action. Each book stands alone, but when used together, they create a system that transforms how you think, plan, and perform in selling – and, more importantly, how you generate meaningful, sustainable revenue.

The marketplace doesn't reward activity. It rewards results. This series is your guide to becoming a true results-driven professional – someone who doesn't just talk about sales but delivers revenue, consistently and relentlessly.

AUTHORS NOTE

When I first got into sales, I thought it was simple: make calls, set meetings, close deals. Like many, I thought revenue would follow if I just worked hard enough. What I learned – the hard way – is that while effort is critical, effort without focus, without a plan, and without a system will only get you so far.

Revenue isn't an accident. It's the outcome of precision, discipline, and relentless execution.

It's the product of building a real sales process – not just hoping your energy or your charm will carry you through.

That's why I wrote the four books you will find in the compilation ***Revenue vs. Sales: Winning is a Planned Event.***

This series is not built on theory. It's built on hard-fought lessons from the front lines – selling to small businesses, to Fortune 500 companies, through good markets and bad ones. It's built from my own experience, the experiences of great mentors, and the many teams I've had the privilege of leading and learning from.

Each book in this series is designed to give you the tools I wish I had much earlier in my career:

- ***The Singular Focus*** helps remove the noise and lock onto what matters, revenue

- ***Revenue Boost*** shows how to build a clear plan you can follow and measure.

- ***Straight Up Selling*** provides the techniques that top sellers live by.

- ***People Drive Revenue*** showcases talent systems that deliver results.

This series is for the sellers who want more than participation trophies. It's for the managers and leaders who know that results are what pay salaries, fund innovation, and create opportunity. It's for anyone who understands that revenue is the real goal, and that sales – when done right – is the system that gets you there.

If you take even one idea, one exercise, or one mindset shift from these books and apply it with consistency, you'll be better than you were yesterday. And over time, that's how greatness is built.

Thank you for reading. Now let's get to work.

Mort Greenberg

TABLE OF CONTENTS

Revenue is what every seller, sales manager, company and investor or shareholder would like to generate. However, focusing on building a sterling sales process and system is the first step to driving your revenue. Having a plan in place will sharpen your go to market strategy and create a... "Revenue. Mindset."

BOOK 1

THE SINGULAR FOCUS

100+ TIPS TO MAXIMIZE
YOUR REVENUE

AUTHORS NOTE

This book, The Singular Focus: 100+ Tips to Maximize Your Revenue, is built on real conversations, real lessons, and real hard-earned truths. It's for anyone—regardless of industry or title—who understands that in sales, results are everything. Whether you're new to selling or a seasoned pro, my hope is that this book gives you a few new tools or reminds you of something timeless: when the world changes around you, the fundamentals of selling do not. The seller who stays focused on revenue will always have a place, always have power, and always have a future.

This book is also a tribute. It's dedicated to **Kenny Wachtel**, a mentor to many—including me—whose no-nonsense approach to sales, leadership, and life taught me lessons that I still use every single day. Kenny had a way of cutting through noise, politics, and excuses and getting to the heart of what mattered: did you deliver? Did you drive revenue? Did you lead with integrity? His impact shaped not just my career but the careers of countless others who were lucky enough to work with him, hear his voice across a conference room, or get an unexpected piece of advice scribbled on a sticky note.

The advice in this book is not theoretical. It's not "what might work someday if everything lines up perfectly." It's what works today, tomorrow, and in the hardest markets you will ever face. It's what kept companies alive during the 2008-2009 financial crisis, what kept teams motivated when goals felt impossible, and what helped

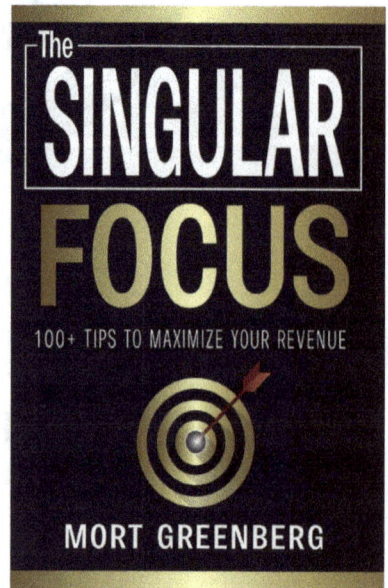

The
SINGULAR
FOCUS
100+ TIPS TO MAXIMIZE YOUR REVENUE

MORT GREENBERG

sellers close deals even when every headwind seemed stacked against them. It's about building a process you can trust, no matter what is happening around you.

Throughout this book, you'll see a common theme: **revenue must be your singular focus**. Not politics. Not effort without results. Not excuses. Revenue. If you stay locked in on that, if you develop the ability to block out distractions and relentlessly pursue the number, you will not only succeed—you will become the kind of professional that companies fight to keep and others aspire to follow.

You'll also see an emphasis on resilience. Getting knocked down is part of the game. Missing a quarter happens. Deals fall through. Budgets get cut. What separates good sellers from great ones isn't just how they celebrate wins—it's how they respond to setbacks. The great ones adapt, evolve, and find a way to get the job done anyway. They version themselves. They stay focused. They do the hard work when no one's watching, and they stay committed to delivering results without losing their sense of service and integrity.

Finally, this book is a reminder that sales is about **relationships and trust**. Long-term success doesn't come from squeezing every dollar out of every deal. It comes from helping clients win. It comes from being someone your customers know will always advocate for them. Sometimes that means leaving a few dollars on the table to close the right deal, the right way. The best deals aren't just the ones that close—they're the ones that renew, that grow, that build a lifetime of business because you did it the right way the first time.

Thank you for picking up this book. Thank you for investing in your craft. And thank you for carrying forward the lessons that mentors like Kenny Wachtel gave to all of us: stay focused, stay relentless, and above all else—deliver.

INTRODUCTION

The introduction sets the stage for the singular focus every seller and sales leader must have: revenue. It shares lessons learned early in the author's career about the importance of asking directly for what you need, staying relentlessly focused on hitting your goals, and building resilience through economic highs and lows. This section reminds readers that no matter how turbulent the environment, results come from focus, preparation, and the discipline to execute against your plan.

In 1996 I was part of a small group that began selling online advertising for Excite.com. Excite.com was one of the first ever Internet media companies, and at that time the leading online "Portal".

For most of us, working at Excite.com was our first or second job. So, we thought of course, we are pretty seasoned business people. I say that with a smile in case you missed it... In 1998 when our company hired a head of all sales we rebelled.

The guy they hired walked in wearing a suit and a tie. We all laughed. This guy obviously was not clued in that we were at a digital media start-up. We were 100% confident we would be teaching our company's new head of sales about well, everything.

However, quickly, as in the first two minutes of this guy in our office, we all hear this voice bellowing out on a conference call with the head of media at AT&T's ad agency.

IF YOU ASK FOR SOMETHING, YOU MIGHT JUST GET IT

The voice from our side told the media director matter-of-factly, "Today is my first day on the job and there is no way you are going to cancel this deal. If you do try and cancel this deal I will call your boss and I will then call the client".

Who the hell is this guy? And maybe I should be wearing a suit too... That day marked the first day that I started taking notes on what this guy was saying. Prior to Excite.com our new head of sales spent 20 years at CBS Television as a head of sales of several divisions there. While at CBS he had led teams that wrote billions of dollars of TV deals with some of the largest brands in America.

Some deals he and his team closed were several hundred million dollars per agreement. Over the next 10-year period of time I would scribble down notes after meeting or talking with my sales mentor KJ. Some sessions were group meetings others were one on one sessions. Bottom-line though, I had a lot to learn and was certainly not seasoned at anything business related after watching this guy operate.

GOOD SELLERS ACHIEVE THEIR GOALS

KJ always had a singular focus on sales goal achievement, and it was in our conversations that I re-learned, and fine- tuned my sales skills. One of my first lessons was that with sales you are only as good as achieving your number. That can be monthly, quarterly or any structure your company has in place. As KJ would say, if you want to get paid the big dollars, and be the head of sales you need to hit your numbers, period.

EVEN IN TURBULENT TIMES YOU CAN BEAT YOUR NUMBER

In 2008/2009, the historic decline of media revenue I was missing digital revenue targets at a start-up inside of NBC Universal's Local TV station group. Hardly was I alone, this was happening all across the advertising industry, but some companies were still making their numbers. What could these companies be doing that I was not?

In an effort to figure it all out in July 2009 I reached out to KJ. Figured if there was one person who would set me straight and get me back on track he would be the one. The hope was to have a quick chat, get some help and talk through the problems I was having.

Turns out I got more than just a good conversation. Over a three- week window of time we had two, multi-hour sit down conversations, plus some homework on my side. These conversations hammered home not only the basics of selling, but of the mindset people need to have to deliver on anything related to revenue.

Regardless of what product you sell KJ's advice holds true, and below are the conversation highlights. At the bottom of this write- up are other one-liners from KJ over the previous years. These other notes I found on post-its and back pages of several notebooks.

"

As KJ would say, if you want to get paid the big dollars, and be the head of sales you need to hit your numbers, period.

"

TABLE OF CONTENTS

THE FIRST CONVERSATION "WHAT IS YOUR PLAN?"

Section 1 emphasizes the importance of creating and executing a clear plan. It dives into why sellers must lock in on revenue as their sole focus and avoid distractions that dilute performance. It stresses that while effort is important, results are the true currency of success. This section offers practical guidance on how to build a strategy around your number, prioritize your selling activities, manage up to leadership, and own every piece of your pipeline with intentionality and urgency. Success starts with a plan—and success is measured by what you deliver.

Revenue is The Singular Focus

1 The best sellers and sales managers need to have a singular focus on revenue. You cannot get lost on too many things.

2 If you are slipping on revenue, you need to determine what you want to do and where you spend your time.

3 If you are better at strategy than sales, fine, but sales pays more.

4 To be great at sales, sellers and managers need to only focus on the number, get better at putting the blinders on to go after the number. Focusing only on the number will keep you in sales.

5 Always know what accounts you need to hit your number, who your sellers are and what motivates them, and how you are going to get the job done...

Results Pay More Than Effort

6 It is not just about keeping the trains running on time, it is about avoiding a train wreck, you have to hit the number.

7 Need to always set the expectation of where the quarter will end up, and need to find a way, no matter what, to deliver the number.

8	Need to have laser focus on selling. Need to fully concentrate on delivering the number.
9	It is not just about working hard, it is about results
10	Need to tell your boss what you need, always keep asking, then if they don't deliver and you miss the number, bring out the docs showing what you asked for.
11	Never get slowed down on what you need, ask for it. Don't get lost on ops, marketing, finance, whatever, tell the boss where the problems are and what you need to drive revenue.
12	Also, don't do your bosses job and tell them what they should be doing. Do your job and tell them what you need to sell more.
13	Need to be great in board meetings. Need to tell them how you are getting the job done, what your wins are, who your best people are, and what they are doing for the organization.
14	Great sellers at times may hit you in the face instead of being nice to you, but that is what it takes.
15	You can't go off in many directions, need to have focus, laser focus on the number.
16	Only 3 things matter: Your goal, your booked revenue and the revenue you need to bring in to close the gap.
17	If you can't deliver the number, need to find a number 2 that can.

18 40 out of 100 people are great sellers and sales managers, but only 5 out of 100 are great strategy people that can see around the corners.

19 Don't get distracted, YOU MUST focus on the number. You MUST deliver the number.

20 Need to be able to go in and tell your boss what you are going to do to close the gap and hit your number.

21 Your boss needs to have the confidence in you that you can deliver, and know that they can believe you can do the job.

22 If you are not able to hit the number you need to tell everyone why, and change what is happening so that you can hit the number.

23 Everyone probably likes you, knows you work hard, but all bosses want is for you to deliver the number.

24 Need to hire great people. You can't have any misses on the hiring front, ever. As soon as someone does not work out, fire them.

25 Don't micro manage, give people room to do their job, but hold them accountable to their number and how they are going to hit it.

26 50,000 foot view, 20,000 foot view, 5 foot view. It is rare for anyone to have all, if you do you will be great.

27 Need to want to mix it up at the 10-yard line and get dirty.

28 When needed you have to get to the client with your seller or in place of your seller, take over the meeting or the deal and get it done

29   No matter what it takes you have to get the deal done.

30   Also you have to be good at the white board.

31   Need to have the strategy piece. Strategy without great selling is death, selling without great strategy is not preferred, but if you hit the number you have achieved the more difficult part of the equation.

32   Don't move jobs to avoid problems you are running into with your role. Pick the right job that matches your skill set, and do that.

33   If you want to do a different job than what you are good at, you need to figure out a way to greatly improve on your weakness so it becomes a strength.

THE SECOND CONVERSATION "COMMUNICATION IS SURVIVAL"

Section two highlights that in addition to focus, communication is a survival skill in sales leadership. It's not enough to work hard—you must constantly manage expectations upward and downward, projecting confidence even under pressure. This section teaches how to manage your boss, how to deliver honest forecasts without undermining your leadership, and why maintaining positivity and owning your number are critical to personal and organizational success. It also drives home the mindset required to push through obstacles: visualizing success, executing without excuses, and solving problems quickly and transparently.

Take Command

and Stay Positive

34   Managing your boss is all about survival.

35   Take command of the number that is achievable.

36   Have to have constructive direction for others, especially the boss on how to hit the number.

37   Have to say the number is not achievable with as much advance warning as possible. Plenty of time allows the organization to best manage costs and profitability.

38   Bosses need to run their business and lower sales revenue means less companywide spending and access to resources.

39   Companies need to have time to plan if revenue is not where they need it to be

40   Survival at the top is about reaching the goal. If you can't hit the #, then tell them.

41   Need a number 2 to manage down to the troops, you need to be the one to manage up in the head of sales role. Need to have the right staff to get the job done.

42   Owning the number is a full-time job and so is managing up. In small companies, you have to do both, but hitting the number is what it is all about.

43 Internet sales are complicated. Only when the organization gets bigger can you afford to have a day-to-day sales leader and an overall head of sales.

44 Don't talk negatively, ever. Always tell your boss you can do the job. Project confidence. If you give anyone a negative, they are going to take what you say as a negative and not have confidence in you.

FOCUS – Own Your Number, Deliver Your Number

45 You can't get distracted, ever!

46 #1 thing the VP of Sales owns is getting to the number, and delivering this to the boss and the board.

47 Manage how you get to the number.

48 Strategy does not count at first, just sales and revenue. After 4 quarters of hitting the number then you can think about the broader strategy, but you have to earn that right.

49 Need to know how to dial back the number.

50 You have to own the number all the time. You need to go to sleep thinking about the number, and how you will get there, and what deals you need to hit the number.

#1 PRIORITY – Always Focus
On Selling. Always

51 Make sure all of your hours are spent focusing on the number. Do not spend time on anything else, if you do, you are not focusing on the only item that matters.

52 If you find you are spending long hours and working hard, but missing your number, you are wasting your time.

53 Always know where you put all your time, and make sure it is all on sales.

54 Need to do core job first, sell the products your company offers.

55 Always think, "Will my boss sleep soundly knowing I'm the right person?"

BE DETERMINED –
Visualize. Execute. Repeat.

56 "I will not fail" No matter what"

57 "I'm going to hit the number, no matter what"

58 Always tell the boss you will hit the number.

59 "Get to where you need to be... No matter what"

60 Look at what is working, look at the inventory you have. Replicate what is working and make sure you have enough inventory to hit the number, or find other ways to get more inventory or products to hit your number. Don't give up, get creative.

61 Know what big deals need to close to hit the number.

62 Know what is needed to get done and delivered every quarter. Quarter after quarter after quarter.

63 Always ask for the deal!! Make sure you are creative enough to secure the deal and not lose it to another.

Find Problems. Solve Problems. Communicate.

64 Own and deliver the #, this is the reality, it is about the number.

65 You can't be distracted in your effort to hit the number.

66 Do the action by walking the walk. Do not just talk the talk.

67 You have to be realistic. What number will close? Always know where your number will come in.

68 Always tell people if there is a problem with your number.

69 Lastly, if you are going to be good at sales you have to change your orientation. Bottom line, manage your number and deliver quarter after quarter after quarter.

70 If you are not able to deliver your number yourself, hire the person that will.

BEYOND YOUR NUMBER

The final section steps back and looks at the broader responsibilities that come with leadership and long-term career growth. It addresses the importance of thinking and acting strategically, managing your career like a business, and hiring and leading others with clarity and strength. Topics range from personal finance to hiring practices to leadership principles and deal-making best practices. The section closes by reinforcing a simple but powerful truth: the best sellers and leaders never lose sight of their number, but they also build strong relationships, foster loyalty, and maintain a long-term perspective in everything they do.

If read this far you probably found a few items that resonated with you. Or you might have started piecing together your plan on how you will continue improving your progress to beating your sales target. With a little bit of focus, communication and effort you will be able to easily push past any obstacle in front of you.

And... As promised, below are a series of one liners and advice I found scribbled in the back of notebooks, on sticky notes and 3x5 cards that I had been saving over the years...

On Being the Head of Sales

71 If you get the VP sales job you had to act senatorial. If you want the CRO or EVP job you need to act presidential.

Always Look Out For You

72 Personal finance is the #2 most important job that you have in your life other than being your own executive recruiter, which is your #1 job.

On Contractors

73 To find people that you trust and show up on time is almost impossible. People never do it at cost they promise.

Common Sense HR

74 Getting a job is not a sprint, it is a marathon. Fast and quick is not as important as making the right decision.

75 Don't want to be looked upon as a non- content when looking for another role inside of your current company.

76 When people want to hire you, they are on their best behavior. It is like dating, people's behavior will never get better than when on the first dates. So, if a hiring manager is a jerk early on, they will only get worse once you are hired. So, avoid that job and find one with a great hiring manager.

77 Defending your people is a big part of being a boss, it needs to be a strong card.

78 When someone asks you to take a new job at your current company, it is either that they want to reward you or get you out of the way. You need to figure out which one and why.

79 Need to come up with good negatives when providing references for people. Ex. They work too hard and never take vacation.

80 Don't go to work for the best buggy whip manufacturer when everyone is driving cars.

81 Always talk to people who want to talk to you (Maybe you will find your next promotion or bigger job).

Leadership

82 Need to live up to your word.

83 Have to follow gut if your gut is always right.

84 90% of getting the job done is in the preparation. The other 10% is showing the company that you can execute against what you have presented to them.

85 The head of sales primary job is to keep the trains running on time.

86 Focus on business maturity.

87   Get the job done. If you are planning on getting to 3rd base, why not put the plan together and run all the way home.

88   It's not about being the smartest in the room—it's about making the smartest people in the room feel heard.

89   A leader's credibility is earned in the moments when no one is watching.

90   If you want to be trusted with the future, start by mastering the now.

91   Leaders aren't judged by ideas—they're judged by impact.

92   Never ask someone to do something you haven't been willing to do yourself.

93   Every time you overpromise, you mortgage your team's morale.

94   Don't just manage results—lead the energy that creates them.

95   A good leader builds a plan. A great leader builds belief.

96   The best way to predict performance is to measure preparation.

Deal Making

97   Need to deliver the number.

98 You will never lose a deal sitting across the table from someone.

99 You always want your client to be happy, even if you have to leave a few dollars on the table to get the deal done.

100 Need to have the drive to always chase the number, and always know where you are against the number.

101 Once a commodity, there is no pricing power.

102 Train is driven by inventory.

103 You don't win deals with discounts—you win them with clarity, confidence, and speed.

104 A great deal is when both sides walk away thinking they got the better end.

105 Don't negotiate to win—negotiate to win again.

106 Pipeline is potential, but deals are proof.

107 You're not in the deal business if you don't know how to walk away.

108 It's not the best product that wins—it's the best positioned, best timed, and best delivered.

109 If urgency isn't built in, the deal will die on someone else's timeline.

110 You can't fake follow-up. Deals are closed in the details.

111 Commodities compete on price; trusted partners compete on value.

112 If you don't control the deal flow, you'll always be reacting to someone else's strategy.

Closing Thought

113 Sometimes it is more about what you / they don't say.

CONCLUSION

At the end of the day, sales is a simple business—but it is not an easy one. It requires relentless focus, constant execution, and the courage to stay centered on what truly matters: delivering revenue. When you strip away the noise, the meetings, and the distractions, success comes down to whether you can consistently identify the right opportunities, put in the right work, and close the deals that drive your number forward.

Throughout this book, you've seen that results aren't an accident. They are the outcome of preparation, focus, communication, and resiliency. The best sellers and sales leaders never drift from the fundamentals. They build a plan. They work that plan. They adapt when needed. And most importantly, they stay committed to the singular goal of delivering results, no matter what challenges stand in the way.

The lessons shared here are not theories—they are battle-tested truths learned over decades of real-world experience and reinforced during good markets and tough downturns alike. They are reminders that true professionalism in sales comes from owning your number, solving problems quickly, leading with confidence, and never losing sight of the relationships you are building along the way. Revenue follows those who consistently focus on delivering value and outcomes for their customers and their organizations.

As you move forward, keep coming back to these ideas. Revisit them when things are going well and when things get tough. Stay focused, stay disciplined, and stay determined. If you do, you won't just beat your number—you'll build a reputation as someone who can be counted on to deliver, year after year, in any environment. And that will be the foundation for a career of lasting success.

FURTHER READING

INTRODUCTION
(Focus on Mental Toughness, Discipline, and Goal Setting)

- *Atomic Habits* by **James Clear** (Master the science of building better habits, essential for staying consistent with revenue-focused behaviors.)

- *Grit* by **Angela Duckworth** (A powerful exploration of why passion and perseverance often matter more than talent when driving results.)

- *The Obstacle Is the Way* by **Ryan Holiday** (A modern take on Stoic philosophy; teaches resilience and how to turn challenges into opportunities.)

- *Relentless: From Good to Great to Unstoppable* by **Tim Grover** (A tough-love manual on the relentless mindset needed to consistently achieve and exceed goals.)

- *Can't Hurt Me* by **David Goggins** (An intense guide to mental toughness and self-discipline, reinforcing the idea that mindset can break any barrier.)

SECTION #1: "WHAT IS YOUR PLAN?"
(Focus on Sales Strategy, Planning, and Execution)

- *The Sales Acceleration Formula* by **Mark Roberge** (A data-driven, process-oriented playbook for building scalable sales organizations.)

- *SPIN Selling* by **Neil Rackham** (One of the most foundational sales books ever written on asking better questions and structuring deals.)

- *New Sales. Simplified.* by **Mike Weinberg** (A step-by-step guide for creating a focused, prospecting-driven sales plan that delivers real revenue.)

- *The Qualified Sales Leader* by **John McMahon** (Focuses on how sales leaders and managers must build and enforce a plan based on rigorous qualification and forecasting.)

- *The Challenger Sale* by **Matthew Dixon and Brent Adamson** (How the best sellers are the ones who teach, tailor, and take control of the sale—perfect for learning to think differently about sales strategy.)

SECTION #2: "COMMUNICATION IS SURVIVAL" (Focus on Leadership, Communication, Managing Up, and Resilient Selling)

- *Dare to Lead* by **Brené Brown** (A must-read on courageous leadership, authentic communication, and fostering trust in teams and organizations.)

- *Crucial Conversations* by **Kerry Patterson, Joseph Grenny, Ron McMillan, and Al Switzler** (Teaches how to communicate effectively and persuasively under high-stakes, high-pressure conditions.)

- *Never Split the Difference* by **Chris Voss** (A masterclass in negotiation and communication techniques from a former FBI hostage negotiator—perfect for high-stakes selling and deal-making.)

- *Radical Candor* by **Kim Scott** (How to communicate feedback and expectations with honesty and care—essential for managing teams and bosses alike.)

- *Leadership and Self-Deception* by **The Arbinger Institute** (Teaches how self-awareness, empathy, and ownership transform communication and leadership effectiveness.)

BOOK 2

REVENUE BOOST

THE ULTIMATE SALES PLAN
IN FIVE STEPS

AUTHORS NOTE

Early in my career the Silicon Valley corporate world that openly embraced me always placed business school graduates in the top jobs. Looking closer at how these grads operated two items jumped out: First, they were great listeners, highly analytical, and asked the best questions. Second, they were great managers of their time, and no matter how hard they worked they always found ways to take vacations, and not work on the weekends.

For me, business school was never going to be in the cards. So the next best thing was to learn as much as possible from business school graduates who attended Harvard, Stanford, Wharton, Columbia, and more.

Week after week, part of the challenge set in my head was that no one would put in more hours than I would. Many nights that meant being in the office until 10 PM or later, and half- day Saturdays and Sundays at a minimum.

This to me was the only way to get ahead of my co-workers, and to continually find more customers and generate more revenue. Canceling planned vacations happened all too often but my view was that I was in learning mode.

For a few years, I worked for NBC Universal while General Electric owned the company. Each year we had a four-phase planning effort that ran throughout the year: Session C in February, with the

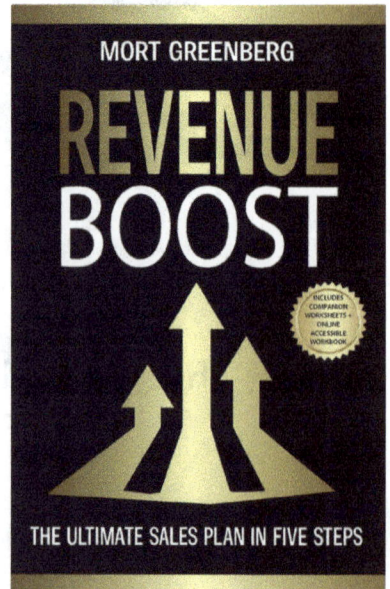

MORT GREENBERG

REVENUE BOOST

INCLUDES COMPARISON WORKSHEETS + ONLINE ACCESSIBLE WORKBOOK

THE ULTIMATE SALES PLAN IN FIVE STEPS

Chairman of each business unit to review each employee and the business overall, Session 1 (S1) in May, to review performance so far in the year, Session 2 (S2) in September, to see how the year would finish and Growth Playbook (GPB) in October, to build next year's expansion plan. The cadence to make planning part of every quarter during the year paid dividends in our growth and ability to stay ahead of the competition.

Every Fall, most companies begin a strategic planning process for the next calendar year. They may not run a process as involved as NBC and GE, but they do put in the effort. Wondering how to create the simplest but most impactful plan is part of where the idea for this book came from. My eagerness to keep learning from anyone that would talk with me about strategic planning has never faded. Paul Gardi and Johnsie Garrett, in many ways this book was made possible because of the time and effort you spent with me over many years. First, you showed me how to bring together objectives, goals, strategies, measures, and tactics. Then you helped me understand each word that goes into the OGSMT is critically important and should be questioned.

This book is built in the form of a workbook. The goal of this workbook is to provide a path to create a simple, but detailed plan to beat your revenue target. These steps can also be used to create a strategic plan for departments beyond sales. However, in a world where sellers must focus on providing customers with the best service and at the same time deliver on their revenue targets, getting lost in planning is rarely an option. This is a do-it-yourself, write in the book to get your ideas on paper. Then scan the QR code to copy the Google Sheets Workbook to your Google Drive and type up your new plan.

INTRODUCTION

Overview of the Five Step Revenue Boost Program

Success in sales is not a mystery; it's a repeatable, measurable process. The Revenue Boost Program was built to help you transform your sales operation – whether you're an individual contributor, a team leader, or an executive – into a high-performing, revenue-generating machine. This book is designed as a playbook and a workbook, so you can take immediate action and build a better future for yourself and your business.

The five steps of the Revenue Boost Program are simple in structure but powerful in effect:

1. **The Survey** – Before you make assumptions, gather direct input. Talk to your customers, your team, and your market to identify what's working, what's not, and where hidden opportunities lie.

The Five Step Process > Series Of One Sheets

Survey → Business Canvas → Competitor Grid →

2. **Business Canvas** – Map out your business model on one page. Define your specialties, your customers, your vendors, your resources, and your growth opportunities. Clarity drives focus; focus drives results.

3. **Competitive Factors** – Know your battlefield. Benchmark yourself against your top competitors based on measurable factors – not opinions – and identify where you must improve to win.

4. **The SWOT Analysis** – Systematically list your strengths, weaknesses, opportunities, and threats. This sharpens your strategy and reveals the blind spots that could sink your success.

5. **OGSMT Plan (Objectives, Goals, Strategies, Measures, Tactics)** – Pull it all together onto one page: what you want to achieve and how you will achieve it. This becomes your living, breathing operating plan for the year ahead.

SWOT OGSMT

Please scan the QR code to access the google sheets and excel workbooks. For google sheets, the file is in "view" mode so choose "file", "copy", and then save to your G Drive to edit

Unlike most sales books that stop at motivational pep talks or generic advice, the Revenue Boost Program shows you exactly how to organize your thinking, structure your strategy, and execute relentlessly – using worksheets, real-world examples, and battle-tested methods.

You will not only hit your revenue goals – you will also build a durable foundation for growth, leadership, and future success.

This is more than a sales plan. It's a revenue mindset upgrade – and it's the mindset that separates the good from the truly great.

Why You Should Have a Written Sales Plan

There's a simple truth that elite performers in every industry understand:

If it's not written down, it's not real.

Too many sales teams and individuals drift from quarter to quarter without a real plan – chasing urgent deals, reacting to the market, hoping for a great year. But hope is not a strategy. And in a competitive world, those who plan, win.

A written sales plan gives you:

- **Clarity:** You know exactly what you are trying to achieve and how you'll get there.

- **Focus:** You can prioritize the work that moves the needle, rather than getting lost in busywork.

- **Accountability:** With clear objectives and milestones, you and your team can measure progress, spot issues early, and course-correct in time.

- **Alignment:** Teams that write and share their sales plans create shared understanding – every person pulling in the same direction.

- **Confidence:** When you plan your work and work your plan, you build the internal certainty that you can achieve what you set out to do.

Think of a written plan as your **GPS for success**. Without it, you're guessing at every intersection. With it, even when conditions change, you can reroute intelligently and stay on course.

Sales is about winning hearts, minds, and deals – but it's also about winning the battle of execution. A written plan transforms strategy from a vague idea into a daily operating system.

Write fast. Plan smart. Execute relentlessly. That's how you beat your goals, your competition, and even your own expectations.

In the pages ahead, you'll learn exactly how to create a sales plan that doesn't gather dust on a shelf – but becomes the engine behind your best year ever.

TABLE OF CONTENTS

REVENUE.
MINDSET.

THE SURVEY

Making Everyone Feel Like an Insider

It all start with Listening, Not Assumptions. Every winning sales plan begins not with strategy – but with listening. Too many leaders build plans based on assumptions instead of real-world input. In this step, you'll gather critical feedback from your customers, employees, and partners, uncovering truths you can't afford to miss. The Survey step is where your strongest growth insights often emerge. The better you listen now, the sharper and more effective your final plan will be. Get ready to turn voices into victories.

Prepare Your Team
for Sales Planning

Before you jump into planning the future, you need to ground yourself in reality — and the best way to do that is by asking your team and your customers for their honest feedback.

■ The simple truth: **people support what they help create**.

When you invite your employees and customers into the planning process, you do two powerful things at once:

- You get valuable, front-line intelligence that leadership alone can't see.

- You foster buy-in, energy, and collaboration that will carry through to execution.

Here's how to prepare your team:

1. Announce the Plan:

Let your employees know you are kicking off a strategic planning process. Frame it positively: *"We want everyone's input so we can build a stronger future together."*

2. Set Expectations:

Explain that you will send around a short survey. Tell them:

- Every voice matters.

- Results will be shared internally.

- Their insights will influence next year's strategy.

3. Promise Transparency:

Commit to sharing the survey results and follow-up actions – this builds trust and creates a culture of openness.

4. Create Excitement:

Position this as an opportunity for each person to shape the team's success, not just another task to complete.

TIP: Create a short kickoff video or host a 10-minute town hall meeting to introduce the survey. Enthusiasm is contagious.

Capturing Survey Data

You have multiple options for collecting survey responses quickly and easily:

- **Google Forms (Free):** Perfect for fast setup and simple reporting.

- **Typeform (Free + Paid):** Great for beautiful, conversational surveys.

- **SurveyMonkey (Paid):** Ideal for more advanced survey logic or analytics.

What matters most is:

- Keep the survey short (7–10 questions max).
- Allow for anonymous feedback if appropriate.

- Provide both multiple-choice and open-ended questions.

- Send a reminder a few days before the deadline to maximize participation.

TIP: Use a survey tool that automatically exports to Excel or Google Sheets for easier analysis later.

Example Survey Questions

Here's a starting point to customize your survey questions for both customers and employees:

Customer Survey Questions

1. What do you like most about our product(s) or service(s)?

2. What improvements would you like to see?

3. How would you rate your overall customer experience?

4. Where do we outperform our competitors?

5. Where do competitors outperform us?

6. What new products or services would you like us to offer?

7. What's the #1 reason you would recommend us – or not?

8. How well do our solutions deliver on your expectations?

9. If you could change one thing about our company, what would it be?

10. Any other feedback you'd like to share?

Employee Survey Questions

1. What do you like most about working here?

2. Where do we need to improve as a company?

3. What tools or support do you need to do your job better?

4. Which competitors do you think we should be most worried about?

5. Where are we beating our competitors?

6. What customer feedback do you hear most often?

7. What new products, services, or ideas should we explore?

8. What obstacles prevent us from growing faster?

9. How can leadership better support your success?

10. If you were CEO for a day, what is the first change you would make?

TIP: Include an optional *"Other comments?"* question at the end – often, the best insights come from the free-form answers.

FOLD BLANK SHEET OF PAPER IN A HALF

Customer Questions	Employee Questions
1. _____	1. _____
2. _____	2. _____
3. _____	3. _____
4. _____	4. _____
5. _____	5. _____

Once you've collected your surveys, don't let the data sit in a file. Act on it.

Here's your four-step process:

1. Identify Common Themes:

Look for repeated answers. If 30% of customers ask for better reporting, that's a red flag. If 40% of employees request more training, that's a growth opportunity.

2. Prioritize Feedback:

Sort the feedback into three categories:

- Critical (must address immediately)
- Important (plan to address soon)
- Nice to have (address later if time/resources allow)

3. Summarize Findings:

Create a one-page snapshot of what you learned. Keep it simple: key themes from customers and employees side-by-side.

4. Share Transparently:

Present the key takeaways to your team. Acknowledge the good, the bad, and the opportunities for improvement. People respect honesty.

TIP: Don't get defensive about negative feedback. Every great company is built on a foundation of continual improvement.

Task #1 — Build and Send Out Your Survey

Here's your action checklist:

- ☐ Draft 7–10 customer survey questions.
- ☐ Draft 7–10 employee survey questions.
- ☐ Choose your survey tool (Google Forms, Typeform, SurveyMonkey, etc.).
- ☐ Write a short intro message explaining the "why" behind the survey.
- ☐ Set a 7–10 day deadline for submissions.
- ☐ Send a friendly reminder 48 hours before the deadline.
- ☐ Review and prioritize the feedback.
- ☐ Summarize results into clear themes.
- ☐ Share findings with your full team.

Congratulations – once you complete this, you'll have **real, authentic insight** to power the rest of your revenue boost plan.

Workshop Activities

Activity 1: Survey Question Brainstorm

Get your leadership team together for 30 minutes.

- Each person must suggest 2–3 survey questions for customers and employees.
- Vote on the top 7–10 questions to finalize.

Activity 2: Run a "Mini Survey" Live

If time allows, run a 5-question live survey in your next team meeting before sending out the full survey. This warms up the team to the idea and builds momentum.

Activity 3: Roleplay Survey Review

After results come in:

- Assign small groups to analyze different sections of feedback.
- Each group presents 3 key insights to the larger team.
- End with a quick brainstorming session: *"What top 3 actions should we take based on this feedback?"*

Conclusion

You Listened. Now You Lead. By completing the Survey step, you've done something most businesses skip – you listened first. You now hold real-world insights that will sharpen every decision you make. The answers you gathered will give you an unbeatable edge because your strategy won't be based on guesses – it will be based on **truths from the people you serve.**

Armed with these insights, you're ready to build a business model that's laser-focused on real needs, real gaps, and real opportunities. **Next up: we'll put it all together on one powerful page – your Business Canvas.**

BUSINESS CANVAS

Your Entire Business, on One Page

Clarify Your Business Model on One Page. If you can't explain your business simply, you don't understand it well enough. The Business Canvas forces you to strip away the noise and focus on the nine essential elements that power your growth: your specialty, your customers, your vendors, your opportunities, and your revenue streams. This canvas will become the foundation for all your strategic choices — what you build, what you sell, and where you grow. One page. Total clarity. Maximum impact.

Nine Elements of
Your Business Canvas

> **"**
>
> *In business — and in battle — clarity wins.*
>
> **"**

The Business Canvas is a simple but transformational tool: a one-page map that forces you to articulate exactly how your business creates value, competes, and grows. Whether you're a founder, a sales leader, or an individual contributor, seeing your business clearly on a single page will unlock better focus, smarter strategy, and faster decision-making.

There are nine essential elements you must define:

Business Specialty	Why Customers Work With You	Key Vendors
What is your core focus?	What unique value do you offer?	Who are your critical partners?
Key Customer Segments	**Relationship Customers Want**	**Key Resources**
Who are your most important audiences?	How do your customers want to interact with you?	What assets power your business — and where are the gaps?
Growth Areas	**Cost Structure**	**Revenue Streams**
Where can you expand?	What are your major costs?	How do you make money today — and how else could you?

1. Business Specialty

What is your core focus?

What specific products, services, or solutions do you deliver better than anyone else?

Example:

A digital ad agency specializing in programmatic advertising for B2B technology firms.

2. Why Customers Work With You

What unique value do you offer?

Why do your customers choose you instead of your competitors? Think beyond price – think experience, innovation, trust, outcomes.

Example:

"We integrate marketing strategy and execution in a way that reduces client workload and accelerates ROI."

3. Key Vendors

Who are your critical partners?

Identify external companies or suppliers who help you deliver your value proposition. This could include software platforms, manufacturers, logistics providers, or consultants.

Example:

Amazon AWS for hosting infrastructure, HubSpot for marketing automation.

4. Key Customer Segments

Who are your most important audiences?

Define your primary customer groups by industry, size, geography, buying behaviors, or needs.

■ **Example:**

Mid-sized healthcare systems in North America, focused on improving patient communication.

5. Relationship Customers Want

How do your customers want to interact with you?

Transactional? Consultative? Automated? High-touch personal service?

■ **Example:**

Enterprise clients expect quarterly strategic reviews and monthly performance check-ins.

6. Key Resources (Have & Need)

What assets power your business — and where are the gaps?

Think in terms of people, technology, intellectual property, brand reputation, funding, or operational systems.

■ **Example:**

Current strength: SEO team.

Needed: Enterprise sales reps in the Southeast region.

7. Growth Areas

Where can you expand?

Identify new products, markets, customer segments, partnerships, or capabilities you must develop to grow revenue.

■ **Example:**

Launching a customer success department to improve retention rates by 20%.

8. Cost Structure

What are your major costs?

Fixed costs (office rent, salaries) and variable costs (ad spend, commissions, platform fees).

■ **Example:**

70% of costs are personnel-related; 15% to technology; 15% to marketing.

9. Revenue Streams

How do you make money today – and how else could you?

Define your current sources of income and identify potential new streams.

■ **Example:**

Current: Subscription SaaS fees.

New Opportunity: Upsell training packages.

■ **TIP:** Don't overcomplicate it. Each box should be filled with short, powerful statements – not paragraphs.

Value of Your Business Canvas

Why bother filling out the canvas? Because:

- **Focus:** You'll see where to direct your limited time, money, and energy.

- **Alignment:** Your team will better understand how their work fits into the big picture.

- **Opportunity spotting:** Gaps and blind spots become obvious when everything's visible at once.

- **Planning Efficiency:** It sets you up perfectly for Step #3 (Competitive Factors) and Step #5 (OGSMT).

Helpful Tip: If you already have a basic P&L (Profit & Loss Statement), review it while building your canvas. It will help you sharpen your answers for Costs and Revenue Streams especially.

Task #2 — Write Your Business Canvas

You're ready to roll up your sleeves. Follow this simple process:

- **Step 1:** Start with your Business Specialty − the heartbeat of everything.

- **Step 2:** Move systematically across all nine elements.

- **Step 3:** Fill in initial answers quickly without overthinking.

- **Step 4:** Review and revise with your leadership team.

- **Step 5:** Finalize Version 1. (You'll probably improve it again later — that's normal!)

Remember: Done is better than perfect for the first pass.

Deep Dive on Each Element (Task Prompts)

	Element	Prompt Question
1	**Business Specialty**	What do we do better or differently than others?
2	**Why Customers Work With You**	What value do we create for them that others don't?
3	**Key Vendors**	Who are our best-fit customers?
4	**Key Customer Segments**	Who are our best-fit customers?
5	**Relationship Customers Want**	What level of communication, service, and personalization do they expect?
6	**Key Resources (Have & Need)**	What assets do we have — and what are we missing?
7	**Growth Areas**	Where could we realistically expand next year?
8	**Cost Structure**	Where does most of our money go?
9	**Revenue Streams**	How are we making money now — and what's next?

Place Your Logo here

BUSINESS SPECIALTY		REASON CUSTOMER WORKS WITH US
What do we do? What is product set?		Which customer problem are we solving?

KEY CUSTOMER SEGMENTS		RELATIONSHIP CUSTOMERS WANT WITH US
From whom are we creating value? Who are our most important customers?		What type of relationship does each customer segment expect us to establish and maintain?

GROWTH AREAS TO DRIVE NEW REVENUE		COST STRUCTURE
What channels, platforms are missing or need improvement?		What are our cost?

BUSINESS CANVAS WORKSHEET
20__

KEY VENDORS

Who are our top suppliers? What activities does each perform

KEY RESOURCES (HAVE AND NEED)

What resources do we need to deliver value to customers? What do we need that we don't have

REVENUE STREAMS

What are our revenue streams?

Tips for Filling Out

Business Canvas Worksheet

- **Be Specific:** Short, clear statements work better than long paragraphs.

- **Prioritize:** Highlight gaps, strengths, and critical areas for growth.

- **Draft First:** You can always refine later — aim for speed over perfection on your first pass.

- **Collaborate:** Share with team members for a richer perspective.

Workshop Activities

Activity 1: Business Canvas Jam Session

- Schedule a 90-minute meeting with your leadership or sales team.

- Create a giant poster-sized Business Canvas or project one on a screen.

- Break into small groups. Each group owns 2–3 boxes to fill out.

- Regroup, review answers together, and refine.

Activity 2: P&L Alignment Review

- Have your CFO or Finance Leader walk the team through the latest P&L.

- As they explain revenue, margins, and costs, update the Revenue Streams and Cost Structure boxes.

Activity 3: Secret Shopper Call

- Assign 2–3 team members to pretend to be a customer or prospect and interact with your sales team or customer service reps.
- Then answer: Is the experience matching the Relationship Customers Want section of your canvas?

Bonus Tip:

Color-code your answers during brainstorming:

- **Green** = Strong
- **Yellow** = Needs Improvement
- **Red** = Missing/Unknown

This helps prioritize where to focus your energy in Step #3 (Competitive Factors) and Step #4 (SWOT).

Conclusion

You See Your Business More Clearly Than Ever. You've just completed something few companies ever take the time to do: You mapped out your business – fully and honestly – on a single page. Now, you know exactly: What you sell. Who you sell it to. How you deliver value.

Where your gaps and opportunities lie. This clarity will give you the focus and discipline to grow faster, smarter, and stronger. Now it's time to move into the arena: understanding your competition and positioning yourself to win.

COMPETITIVE FACTORS

Build a Map to Beat Your Competition

Know Your Battlefield — And Where to Attack. Business isn't played in a vacuum — it's played on a competitive field. In this step, you'll benchmark yourself against competitors on the factors that truly matter to customers. By defining and measuring your position, you'll find new opportunities to outpace rivals, seize market share, and serve customers better than anyone else. You can't win if you don't know the score. Let's measure it — and then beat it.

Define Your Factors of Competition

You can't outperform the competition if you don't know what battlefield you're on — and where your real advantages and vulnerabilities lie.

Competitive Factors are the attributes that matter most to your customers when they decide between you and your competitors.

This step is about defining, measuring, and benchmarking those factors — and then setting clear targets to gain an edge.

―――――― 〝 ――――――

The most dangerous assumption in business is that you know why you're winning... or why you're losing.

―――――― 〟 ――――――

Taking a structured, objective look at your competition removes guesswork and provides a hard-edged blueprint for improvement.

How to Define Your Factors of Competition

Start by asking:

- What do customers care about most when choosing a product or service like ours?

- Where are our competitors currently better than us?

- Where are we better — and by how much?

The best factors are:

- Measurable (quantitative where possible)
- Relevant to the customer decision process
- Actionable (you can improve them)

Common Competitive Factors Examples

(choose based on your business type)

CATEGORY	SAMPLE FACTORS
Digital	Website traffic, conversion rate, time on site, SEO rank, app downloads
Sales	Response time, pricing flexibility, contract terms, payment options
Customer Success	Net Promoter Score (NPS), client retention rates, onboarding speed
Brand	Brand awareness, social media followers, engagement rates, customer reviews
Product	Product reliability, innovation rate, feature richness, customization options
Distribution	Speed of delivery, number of distribution points, ease of purchase
Service	Customer support availability, customer satisfaction scores, self-service options

TIP: Select 5 to 10 critical factors. More than 10 will dilute your focus.

A Quick Example

If you're a SaaS company selling CRM tools, your factors of competition might include:

- Time to onboard a new customer (days)
- Number of integrations available
- Mobile app ratings on iOS/Android stores
- Number of active monthly users (MAUs)
- Cost per user per month

Task #3 — Benchmark with Factors of Competition

Once you define your factors, it's time to measure yourself and your top competitors.

The Benchmarking Process:

1. Identify Top 3 Competitors

- Focus on the ones your customers actually compare you to – not necessarily the biggest brands in the world.
- Competitors could be direct, indirect, or emerging challengers.

2. Gather Data

- Use public data (website traffic tools like SimilarWeb, social media counts, app store ratings, review sites).

- Use customer feedback ("Which competitors did you consider before choosing us? Why?")

- Use mystery shopping – call, email, or interact with competitors pretending to be a prospect.

3. Build Your Competitive Grid

Key Factors	Your Company	Competitor 1	Competitor 2	Competitor 3
Website Traffic (Monthly)	150,000	200,000	180,000	90,000
Avg Response Time (Hours)	2 hours	8 hours	4 hours	1 hours
Customer Satisfaction (NPS)	70	62	77	68
Number of Integrations	40	25	60	30
Pricing Flexibility	High	Medium	Low	High

Highlight where you lead (green)

Highlight where you behind (red)

Competitive Benchmark
Grid Template

Instructions:

- List your company and your top 3 competitors across the top.

- Choose 5–10 critical factors of competition in the left-hand column.

- Fill in the measurable data for each competitor and yourself.

- Highlight strengths and gaps.

Key Competitive Factors	Your Company	Competitor 1	Competitor 2	Competitor 3
1.				
2.				
3.				
4.				
5.				
6.				
7.				
8.				
9.				
10.				

How to Use This Template

List Your Competitors:

These should be the competitors your customers realistically consider when evaluating options.

Choose Critical Factors:

Think about what truly influences a customer's buying decision: speed, pricing, brand reputation, features, customer experience, etc.

Gather Data:

Use public sources (websites, social media, review sites, reports) or direct intelligence (customer feedback, mystery shopping).

Score Objectively:

- Where possible, use hard numbers (e.g., response time in hours, satisfaction score out of 10, cost per unit).
- Where not possible, use standardized scales (e.g., High/Medium/Low).

Color Code:

- Green for areas where you lead
- Red for areas where you're behind
- Yellow for areas you are close to parity but could improve

Take Action:

- Choose 2–3 areas where improvement would make the biggest difference.
- Set improvement goals tied to your OGSMT in Step 5.

Bonus Tip: "Priority Focus Box"

At the bottom of the worksheet, add this simple call-out:

Our Top 3 Priority Improvements Based on Benchmarking:

1. _____

2. _____

3. _____

Fold Blank Sheet of Paper into nine boxes (1/3, 1/3, 1/3)

Competitor 1	*Factor 1*	*Factor 4*
Competitor 2	*Factor 2*	*Factor 5*
Competitor 3	*Factor 3*	*Factor 6*

4. Analyze and Prioritize

- What 2–3 critical areas MUST we improve to win more deals?

- Where can we double down on an existing advantage?

- What new factors are emerging that we must watch?

Why This Step Matters

- You stop guessing why you are winning or losing deals.

- You find opportunities to disrupt competitors before they disrupt you.

- You motivate your team with clear, external benchmarks to beat.

Benchmarking is not about copying competitors — it's about choosing the battles you can win and where you can set the pace.

Workshop Activities

Activity 1: Competitive Factors Brainstorm

- Assemble a team of sales, marketing, customer success, and leadership members.
- Give everyone sticky notes.
- Write down ALL possible factors customers care about.
- Vote as a group to select the Top 7–10 factors that matter most.

Activity 2: Secret Shopper Challenge

- Assign team members to "shop" competitor websites,

social profiles, sales funnels, or customer service reps.

- Each shopper answers:
- How easy was it to find information?
- How fast did they respond?
- What stood out about their customer experience?
- Summarize and add findings to your Competitive Grid.

Activity 3: Battle Card Creation

- Based on your benchmarking, create 1-page Competitive Battle Cards for your sales team:
- Key competitor strengths
- Key competitor weaknesses
- How to position yourself to win head-to-head

Pro Tip

Benchmark again every 6 months. Markets shift. Technology changes. Competitors evolve. The companies that benchmark consistently are the ones that stay ahead.

Conclusion

You Know the Battlefield — and You Know How to Win. Most companies operate in the dark, assuming they know how they stack up against competitors. Not you. You now have a clear, data-driven picture of where you lead, where you lag, and where you can attack. You've benchmarked yourself against the market — and identified your most winnable battles. Next, we'll sharpen your strategic edge even further by doing a full S.W.O.T. analysis: Strengths, Weaknesses, Opportunities, and Threats.

THE S.W.O.T.

Find Your Strengths, Expose Your Gaps, Seize Your Opportunities

Face Reality — And Build from Strength. You can't grow without facing reality. In Step 4, you'll perform a brutally honest S.W.O.T. analysis — capturing your Strengths, Weaknesses, Opportunities, and Threats. This is the step where you expose blind spots, uncover hidden advantages, and identify the biggest moves you must make next. The companies that thrive aren't just good at leveraging their strengths — they're fearless about fixing their weaknesses. See clearly. Act boldly. Build stronger.

List Your Strengths, Weaknesses, Opportunities, and Threats

The S.W.O.T. analysis remains one of the most valuable strategic planning tools in business — because it forces you to think with brutal honesty about where you stand today, both internally and externally.

A great S.W.O.T. gives you:

- Clear visibility into your core strengths you must leverage.

- Exposure of critical weaknesses you must fix.

- Identification of emerging opportunities you must capture.

- Awareness of external threats you must prepare for.

Reality check: Great companies aren't just great because they know what they're good at — they're great because they know what they're bad at and relentlessly work to improve it.

Breaking Down the S.W.O.T.

Area	Definition	Examples
Strengths (Internal)	What do we do well today? What advantages do we have over competitors?	Strong brand loyalty, fastest onboarding time, unmatched domain expertise, strong customer relationships.
Weaknesses (Internal)	What do we struggle with internally that holds us back?	Limited product range, outdated website, low sales productivity, high employee turnover.

Area	Definition	Examples
Opportunities (External)	What favorable trends, gaps, or unmet needs exist in the market?	Growing new customer segment, competitor missteps, emerging technologies, favorable regulations.
Threats (External)	What external risks or changes could hurt us?	New disruptive competitors, market saturation, pricing pressure, changing customer preferences.

How to Conduct
Your S.W.O.T. Analysis

Step 1: Gather the Right Inputs

- Use your customer survey data (Step #1) to identify external insights.

- Use your employee survey data to identify internal realities.

- Use your competitive benchmarking (Step #3) to highlight competitive risks and gaps.

Step 2: Write Fast, Then Refine

- Start by listing bullet points under each category.

- Then prioritize the top 3–5 items for each quadrant.

- Eliminate overlap (e.g., don't list the same item as both a strength and opportunity – be disciplined).

STRENGTHS

INTERNAL

1.

2.

3.

4.

5.

OPPORTUNITIES

EXTERNAL

1.

2.

3.

4.

5.

S.W.O.T.
20__

WEAKNESSES

1.

2.

3.

4.

5.

THREATS

1.

2.

3.

4.

5.

Quick Example of a B2B
Software Company S.W.O.T

Strengths	Weaknesses
• High customer retention rate (90% annually). • Flexible pricing models customers love. • Strong partnerships with complementary platforms.	• Onboarding time is 20% longer than competitors. • Limited brand recognition in Europe. • Sales team turnover 18% annually.
Opportunities	Threats
• New demand for remote workflow tools. • Expansion into the healthcare industry. • Upsell existing clients with add-on modules.	• New competitor offering free basic service. • Increasing regulatory hurdles for data storage. • Growing customer preference for mobile-first solutions.

TIP: Keep S.W.O.T. statements short, sharp, and actionable. Avoid corporate jargon like *"leverage synergies"* – it hides real issues.

Collect Your
S.W.O.T. Input

Here's your action checklist:

- Review your customer survey results – note customer perceptions of strengths, weaknesses, opportunities, threats.

- Review your employee survey results – note internal feedback about what's working and what's broken.

- Review your competitive benchmark grid – note where you're leading, lagging, or vulnerable.

- Assemble your leadership team or department heads for a S.W.O.T. Jam Session.

   Facilitator Tip: Assign one person to lead each section (Strengths, Weaknesses, etc.) to ensure full group engagement.

S.W.O.T. Matrix Worksheet
(Quadrant Style)

Strengths
(Internal, Positive)

1.

2.

3.

Opportunities
(External, Positive)

1.

2.

3.

Weaknesses
(Internal, Negative)

1.

2.

3.

Threats
(External, Negative)

1.

2.

3.

HOW TO USE THIS S.W.O.T. QUADRANT

- Fill out 3–5 bullets in each quadrant.
- Think internal (Strengths and Weaknesses) vs. external (Opportunities and Threats).
- Keep each bullet short, specific, and actionable.
- Prioritize 1–2 key items from each box for your strategic planning.

Bonus Priority Section (Optional Below the Grid)

- Top Strength to Amplify:

_____

- Top Weakness to Fix:

_____

- Top Opportunity to Pursue:

_____

- Top Threat to Defend Against:

_____

This **quadrant layout** mirrors classic strategic planning boards (like what leadership teams use in offsites and workshops) – but it's simplified enough to encourage readers to take action immediately.

Workshop Activities

Activity 1: S.W.O.T. Sticky Note Session

- Set up a whiteboard or virtual board with four quadrants: Strengths, Weaknesses, Opportunities, Threats.
- Give each participant 10–15 sticky notes or virtual cards.
- 5 minutes: silently write down observations (one per note).
- Group the notes into themes. Vote on the top 3–5 for each category.

Activity 2: 5 Whys Drill Down

- Pick 1 Weakness and ask the team *"Why is this true?"*
- Then ask *"Why?"* again for the answer.
- Repeat 5 times.
- You'll often uncover the root cause of major problems instead of treating symptoms.

Example:

"Our customer churn is high." -> Why? -> *"Onboarding is too slow."* -> Why? -> *"Our training materials are confusing."* -> Why? -> *"We haven't updated them in two years."*

Activity 3: Opportunity Radar Exercise

- List the top 5 market trends you see.
- Map those trends to potential Opportunities in your S.W.O.T.
- Challenge your team: "Which of these can we turn into revenue fastest?"

Pro Tip

After completing your S.W.O.T., immediately ask:

- *"Which Strength can we DOUBLE DOWN on?"*
- *"Which Weakness do we have to FIX first?"*
- *"Which Opportunity can we MOVE ON immediately?"*
- *"Which Threat deserves a CONTINGENCY PLAN?"*

This mindset turns the S.W.O.T. from a passive exercise into an action-oriented planning tool.

Conclusion

You Faced Reality – and Built a Better Foundation. You didn't flinch. You looked at your business honestly – strengths, weaknesses, opportunities, and threats – and now you see the full landscape. Your S.W.O.T. gives you the true map of where to double down, where to improve, what to chase, and what to defend against. This isn't just a checklist – it's your strategic edge. When you know yourself, you can play offense with total confidence. Now, you're ready for the final – and most exciting – step: turning all of this insight into an unstoppable action plan with the OGSMT.

THE OGSMT

Your Entire Strategic Plan, on One Page

Turn Insights into Action — On One Page. This is where everything comes together. In Step 5, you'll build your complete revenue plan — your Objectives, Goals, Strategies, Measures, and Tactics — on a single page. The OGSMT is your blueprint for execution: it turns good ideas into daily actions, keeps your team aligned, and ensures you deliver results month after month. With a clear OGSMT, you don't just set goals — you create a living system to achieve them. Plan it. Own it. Crush it.

Put Your Objectives, Goals, Strategies, Measures, and Tactics on One Page

After collecting insights (Survey), clarifying your business model (Canvas), benchmarking the competition (Competitive Factors), and analyzing your current reality (SWOT), you're ready for the final – and most important – step:

The OGSMT.

OGSMT stands for:

- **O**bjectives

- **G**oals

- **S**trategies

- **M**easures

- **T**actics

Together, these five elements form a **living strategic document** that drives clarity, focus, accountability, and growth across your team.

The magic of OGSMT?

- It's structured enough to drive execution.

- It's flexible enough to adapt during the year.

- It fits on a **single page** – ensuring everyone can read and use it.

If you can't fit your plan on one page, it's too complicated to win.

The Five Elements
of Your OGSMT

Objectives	The big-picture accomplishments you seek.
Goals	The measurable targets proving you're succeeding.
Strategies	The broad methods for achieving the goals.
Measures	How you track the effectiveness of the strategies.
Tactics	The specific projects/actions to execute the strategies.

Think of it like this:

- **Objectives and Goals** are the destination.

- **Strategies, Measures,** and **Tactics** are the roadmap and dashboard.

OBJECTIVES	Long term, broad objective(s) - usually to be accomplished over the next year. What we need/want to fulfill madate or mission. Your objectives should be fairly obvious and simple.	Words
GOALS	Covers large, overriding considerations such as Revenue, Share, Volume, and Profit. The spexific results we need to acheve our objective. A specific and actionable definition of what 'success' actually looks like. Must be S.M.A.R.T (Specific, measurable, actionable, realistic, time-bound).	Numbers/date

STRATEGIES	The key 4-5 strategies designed to build the competitive advantage necessary to achieve the goals. How we will aciheve our goals Often take the form of projects or programs. Must make a specific decission or it is not a strategy.	Words
MEASURES	That which tells tou that the strategies are being achieved (specific benchmarks, usually with a one year horizon). Objective and quantifiable. Necessitates data collection. Measures serve as basis for evaluating performance of the organization and of the managers, volunteers, and employees.	Numbers
TACTICS	Specific list of projcets that as completed will bring you closer to achieving your strategies. Each of the 4-5 strategies will have 5-10, or more tactics.	Words

Setting Objectives (What To Accomplish)

When writing Objectives, focus on what must be achieved to move the business forward over the next 12–24 months.

■ **Good Objective Example:**

"Expand into three new regional markets by end of FY."

Checklist for Objectives:

- Ambitious but achievable

- Short, punchy statements

- No jargon

Setting Goals (Revenue / Quantities To Beat)

Your Goals must be **quantitative**. They make success black and white: **you hit the number, or you don't.**

■ **Example Goals:**
- Increase Annual Recurring Revenue (ARR) by $10M.
- Reach a 20% market share in the healthcare vertical.
- Acquire 500 net-new customers by Q4.

TIP:

Break annual goals into quarterly or even monthly checkpoints to keep momentum high.

Setting Strategies (Achieving Objectives + Goals)

Strategies are the **"how"** behind achieving your Goals.

■ **Example Strategies:**
- Launch Account-Based Marketing (ABM) to target top 100 prospects.
- Expand product offering to adjacent verticals.
- Partner with industry associations to gain credibility and leads.

Key Tip:

Strategies must involve real choices. (*"Work harder"* or *"sell more"* is not a strategy.)

Setting Measures (Dates & Metrics of Success)

Measures track whether your strategies are actually delivering results.

Good Measures include:

- Specific quantity targets
- Deadlines or timeframes
- Clear ownership

Example Measures:
- 30% increase in inbound leads within 6 months.
- Improve customer onboarding NPS from 60 to 75 by year-end.
- $3M in new revenue generated by Q3.

Setting Tactics (Actions / Projects To Do)

Tactics are the daily and weekly actions that make strategies real.

Good Tactics Examples:
- Hire 3 new SDRs in Q2.
- Launch new customer referral program by May.
- Develop and deploy new training platform for customer service reps by July.

Best Practice:

Each tactic should have:

- An Owner *(who's responsible)*

- A Due Date *(when it's done)*

Formatting Your OGSMT

Here's the recommended structure:

Element	Definition	Example
Mission	Purpose — Why you exist.	"Empower small businesses to succeed through smarter marketing."
Vision	Future Aspiration — What you want to become.	"Be the #1 marketing platform for small businesses worldwide."
Objectives	Big overarching achievements needed.	Grow revenue by 20% YoY.
Goals	Specific, measurable financial or operational targets.	Achieve $50M in annual revenue. Secure 1,000 new customers.
Strategies	How you will accomplish your objectives.	Launch new product lines, expand into Europe, strengthen customer success.
Measures	Metrics to track progress toward strategies.	Weekly sales meetings, quarterly NPS surveys, monthly pipeline reviews.
Tactics	Projects and action items assigned to owners.	Create outbound prospecting team; roll out customer loyalty program.

How to Write Mission and Vision Statements

Your Mission is your reason for being.

- **Ask:** *"What big purpose do we serve?"*

- Keep it short (1–2 lines).

- Use strong, action-oriented language.

■ Mission Statement Examples:

- **Google:** "Organize the world's information and make it universally accessible and useful."

- **Tesla:** "To accelerate the world's transition to sustainable energy."

- **Boeing:** "Connect, protect, explore, and inspire the world through aerospace innovation."

Your Vision is your aspirational future.

- **Ask:** *"If we do everything right, what does success look like?"*

- Make it bold, inspiring, and forward-looking.

■ Vision Statement Examples:

- **Google:** "Provide access to the world's information in one click."

- **Tesla:** "Create the most compelling car company of the 21st century."

- **TED:** "Spread ideas."

Cascading Your OGSMT – For Larger Companies

If you're leading a large organization, you'll need to cascade the OGSMT. This ensures alignment, ownership, and accountability from the C-Suite to the newest intern.

That means:

- **Corporate-Level OGSMT:** Sets the Mission, Vision, Objectives, and high-level Goals.

- **Department-Level OGSMTs:** Each team creates their own OGSMT that aligns upward.

- **Team or Individual OGSMTs:** Translate department Goals and Strategies into personal workstreams.

CORPORATE LEVEL

MISSION AND VISSION

O **G** S **M** T

A well-cascaded OGSMT ensures that each team's (or an individual's) activities are aligned with the overall organization's objectives and goals

The higher-level organization's **STRATEGY** becomes the lower-level organization's **OBJECTIVE**

DIVISIONAL OR BUSINESS UNIT OR DEPARTMENT

O G S **M** T

The higher-level organization's **MEASURES** becomes the lower-level organization's **GOALS** and so on

TEAM OR INDIVIDUAL

O **G** S M T

O: Objectives | G: Goals | S: Strategies | M: Measures | T: Tactics

Write Your OGSMT

Action Checklist:

- Write a first draft of your Mission and Vision.
- Draft 2–4 key Objectives for the next 12 months.
- Define 3–5 measurable Goals tied to those Objectives.
- Choose 4–6 Strategies to achieve those Goals.
- Set clear Measures and Due Dates for each Strategy.
- List 3–5 Tactics under each Strategy, assign owners and deadlines.
- Fit it all onto one page (or a simple Google Sheet).

■ Rapid Write, Retreat, Repeat:
Your first version won't be perfect — expect 3–5 versions before you nail it.

OGSMT Strategic Plan

Worksheet (Fillable)

MISSION STATEMENT (Purpose)

Why do we exist? What's our ultimate purpose?

_____

_____

_____

VISION STATEMENT (Future Aspiration)

What are we trying to become? What does success look like in the future?

_____

_____

_____

OBJECTIVES (What To Accomplish — Big Themes)

_____

_____

GOALS (Specific, Measurable Targets)

1. _____
2. _____
3. _____
4. _____

STRATEGIES (How You Will Win)

1. _____
2. _____
3. _____
4. _____

MEASURES (Key Metrics + Deadlines)

Strategy	Measure	Target/ Deadline
1. _____	_____	_____
2. _____	_____	_____
3. _____	_____	_____
4. _____	_____	_____

STRATEGIES (How You Will Win)

1. _____
2. _____
3. _____
4. _____

MEASURES (Key Metrics + Deadlines)

1. _____
2. _____
3. _____
4. _____

TACTICS (Projects and Actions)

Tactic	Owner	Due Date
1. _____	_____	_____
2. _____	_____	_____
3. _____	_____	_____
4. _____	_____	_____

Completion Checklist

- Mission and Vision are written clearly.

- Objectives are strategic and directional.

- Goals are measurable and time-bound.

- Strategies are actionable and choiceful.

- Measures define success quantitatively.

- Tactics are assigned to owners with due dates.

Print this template landscape (horizontal) when formatting it into your book or PDF — it makes the one-page readability even sharper!

Now you have a true fillable OGSMT template to complete the full upgraded system!

Would you also like me to create a "Completed Sample OGSMT" next, so readers can see a fully filled-in example before they start drafting their own? (This really boosts success rates because people love to see a working model first!)

EXAMPLE > Completed Sample OGSMT for a Up and Coming Digital Ad Agency

MISSION STATEMENT (Purpose)

Help small and mid-sized businesses grow faster by delivering exceptional digital marketing services.

VISION STATEMENT (Future Aspiration)

Be the most trusted marketing partner for 10,000+ SMBs globally by 2030.

OBJECTIVES (What To Accomplish — Big Themes)

1. Increase market share in core industries (Healthcare, Education, Retail).

2. Improve customer retention and satisfaction rates.

3. Launch two new service offerings in the next 12 months.

4. Strengthen internal team skills through ongoing training and development.

GOALS (Specific, Measurable Targets)

1. Achieve $5M in annual recurring revenue (ARR) by end of year.

2. Reach 85% customer retention rate by Q4.

3. Launch two new services by October 1st.

4. Train 100% of client-facing employees in new service methodologies by December 31st.

STRATEGIES (How You Will Win)

1. Expand sales efforts into underdeveloped regions (Midwest, Southeast US).

2. Enhance onboarding and support programs for new customers.

3. Develop bundled service offerings for upsell and cross-sell.

4. Launch a formal internal training academy.

MEASURES (Key Metrics + Deadlines)

Measures	Target/Deadline
1. Hire 5 new sales reps in Midwest/ Southeast	By June 30
2. Achieve Net Promoter Score (NPS) >70 for onboarding experience	By September 30

Measures	Target/Deadline
3. Launch two bundled service packages	By October 1
4. Conduct 4 quarterly training bootcamps	First bootcamp by March 31

TACTICS (Projects and Actions)

Tactics	Owner	Due Date
1. Create regional sales rep job descriptions and post online	HR Manager	March 15
2. Develop 4-part onboarding email + webinar series	Client Success Director	May 1
3. Design and price bundled service offers (SEO + Paid Media, CRM + Email Marketing)	Product Manager	August 1
4. Develop internal LMS (Learning Management System)	Training Coordinator	July 15
5. Schedule first training bootcamp for new hires for training academy	Training Coordinator	March 31

Highlights From This Completed Sample

- Mission and Vision are aspirational but clear and focused.

- Objectives align with growth, retention, innovation, and team capability.

- Goals are numeric and time-bound (good S.M.A.R.T. format).

- Strategies are real, strategic moves – not generic statements.

- Measures track progress sharply and have specific deadlines.

- Tactics are assignable and immediately actionable.

■ Pro Tip:

After building your OGSMT, schedule a monthly review to track progress on Measures and update Tactics as needed.

This is how it becomes a living operating system – not just a planning document!

Workshop Activities

Activity 1: OGSMT Drafting Blitz

- 1-hour team session.

- Each leader drafts their first pass OGSMT based on survey + canvas + SWOT data.

- Group review to tighten wording, remove redundancies.

Activity 2: "Owner & Date Assignment" Sprint

- After all tactics are listed, assign an Owner and Due Date in real-time.

- If there's no clear owner, the tactic needs revision or clarification.

Activity 3: One-Page Test

- Each team posts their OGSMT on a wall or shared screen.
- If it doesn't fit cleanly onto a single page – trim and prioritize.

■ Pro Tip

- A great OGSMT doesn't just plan the future – it operates the business month after month.
- Review it quarterly and update it at least once a year.

Conclusion

You Don't Just Have a Plan. You Have a System for Success. Congratulations – you've built more than a sales plan. You've built a full, aligned, one-page operating system for revenue growth. With your Objectives, Goals, Strategies, Measures, and Tactics clearly defined, you now have: A blueprint for action. A way to measure success. A system that drives accountability and momentum. This isn't just about planning. It's about executing better, faster, and stronger every day. Now go out there, execute your OGSMT, and build the best year – and the best business – you've ever had.

Your Next Moves

You made it. But this isn't the end. This is the beginning of your next, bigger, better year. Over these five steps, you have built what most businesses dream about — but few actually achieve:

- You listened deeply to your customers, team, and market.

- You mapped your entire business on one clear page.

- You measured yourself honestly against your competition.

- You faced your strengths, weaknesses, opportunities, and threats with courage.

- You built a complete, one-page strategic plan — your OGSMT — ready to guide every decision and drive every win.

You have something powerful now:
Real insight. Real clarity. Real action steps.

The tools you built here aren't just for this quarter or this year. They are repeatable systems you can refresh, refine, and relaunch every year for the rest of your career.

What to Do Next

Here's your action list to keep the momentum going:

1. Activate Your OGSMT Immediately

- Schedule your first team kickoff meeting.
- Share your one-page plan with every key stakeholder.
- Assign early wins and quick-start projects.
- Set up monthly checkpoints to track progress against Measures and Tactics.

■ **Pro Tip:** The faster you activate your plan, the faster you build belief.

2. Build OGSMT Habits into Your Calendar

- Review your OGSMT monthly with your leadership team.
- Update Measures quarterly based on real progress.
- Revise Strategies annually based on market shifts.
- Refresh your full OGSMT every 12 months.

■ **Pro Tip:** Treat your OGSMT like a living system – not a one-time document.

3. Keep Listening

- Repeat customer and employee surveys at least once per year.

- Host quarterly "Voice of the Customer" roundtables.
- Stay curious. Markets shift. Needs evolve. Listening never ends.

Pro Tip: Listening is your permanent competitive advantage.

4. Keep Benchmarking

- Update your Competitive Factors grid every six months.
- Watch new entrants, new technologies, and new threats.
- Set stretch targets to keep yourself ahead of the competition.

Pro Tip: Winning companies measure differently – and act faster.

5. Keep Strengthening Your Foundation

- Use your SWOT analysis not once, but as a living risk-and-opportunity map.
- Celebrate when you turn Weaknesses into Strengths.
- Prepare defense strategies against top Threats.

Pro Tip: SWOT isn't a report card – it's a weapon for smarter, faster decisions.

Final Words: You Are Ready

Success isn't about having the perfect plan. It's about having a **good plan, executed with focus, energy, and relentless improvement**. You now have that plan. You now have that system. You now have the foundation, the map, and the momentum. There's only one thing left to do: **Execute like your future depends on it – because it does**.

And if you have not yet download the workbook, you can scan this QR code. Now go out there. Deliver your best year ever. Lead your team to greatness. And when you reach your goals? Raise the bar – and do it again.

APPENDIX:
FURTHER READING BY SECTION

STEP 1: THE SURVEY
Mastering Listening, Research, and Customer Discovery

- **Rob Fitzpatrick** | *The Mom Test* | CreateSpace Independent Publishing Platform, London, 2013

- **Cindy Alvarez** | *Lean Customer Development* | O'Reilly Media, Sebastopol, CA, 2014

- **Ryan Levesque** | *Ask* | Dunham Books, Austin, TX, 2015

- **Peter Fader** | *Customer Centricity* | Wharton Digital Press, Philadelphia, PA, 2012

- **Matthew Dixon, Nick Toman, Rick DeLisi** | *The Effortless Experience* | Portfolio, New York, NY, 2013

STEP 2: BUSINESS CANVAS
Mastering Business Models and Value Creation

- **Alexander Osterwalder, Yves Pigneur** | *Business Model Generation* | John Wiley & Sons, Hoboken, NJ, 2010

- **A.G. Lafley, Roger L. Martin** | *Playing to Win* | Harvard Business Review Press, Boston, MA, 2013

- **Eric Ries** | *The Lean Startup* | Crown Business, New York, NY, 2011

- **W. Chan Kim, Renée Mauborgne** | *Blue Ocean Strategy* | Harvard Business Review Press, Boston, MA, 2005

- **Alexander Osterwalder, Gregory Bernarda, Alan Smith, Yves Pigneur** | *Value Proposition Design* | John Wiley & Sons, Hoboken, NJ, 2014

STEP 3: COMPETITIVE FACTORS
Mastering Competitive Analysis and Strategic Benchmarking

- **Michael E. Porter** | *Competitive Strategy* | Free Press, New York, NY, 1980

- **Rita McGrath** | *Seeing Around Corners* | Houghton Mifflin Harcourt, Boston, MA, 2019

- **John Doerr** | *Measure What Matters* | Portfolio, New York, NY, 2018

- **Richard Rumelt** | *Good Strategy Bad Strategy* | Crown Business, New York, NY, 2011

- **Patrick Bet-David** | *Your Next Five Moves* | Gallery Books, New York, NY, 2020

STEP 4: THE S.W.O.T.
Mastering Internal Analysis and Strategic Self-Awareness

- **Tom Rath** | *StrengthsFinder 2.0* | Gallup Press, New York, NY, 2007

- **Kim Scott** | *Radical Candor* | St. Martin's Press, New York, NY, 2017

- **William T. Brooks** | *Playing Bigger Than You Are* | McGraw-Hill Education, New York, NY, 2009

- **Tony Robbins** | *Awaken the Giant Within* | Free Press, New York, NY, 1991

- **Bernard Boar** | *The Art of Strategic Planning for Information Technology* | John Wiley & Sons, New York, NY, 1999

STEP 5: THE OGSMT
Mastering Execution, Strategic Planning, and Goal Achievement

- **Chris McChesney, Sean Covey, Jim Huling** | *The 4 Disciplines of Execution* | Free Press, New York, NY, 2012

- **Verne Harnish** | *Scaling Up* | Gazelles, Inc., Ashburn, VA, 2014

- **Michael Hyatt** | *Your Best Year Ever* | Baker Books, Grand Rapids, MI, 2018

- **Cameron Herold** | *Vivid Vision* | Greenleaf Book Group Press, Las Vegas, NV, 2018

- **James Clear** | *Atomic Habits* | Avery, New York, NY, 2018

Thank you for reading,
and here's to your ongoing success!

BOOK 3

STRAIGHT UP SELLING

YOUR SALES TOOLBOX FOR EXCELLENCE

AUTHORS NOTE

Selling Can be Like Art

There is no question, like you, I love selling. Each day presents unique challenges and like a blank canvas you can fill it in as the right inspiration comes to you. For 25+ years, coming up with new solutions for customers is part of the joy of selling, hopefully, you feel the same.

Over the years I have written down various hacks and tips to help me continually improve as a seller and sales manager. Along the way, these nuggets became training segments that were tested over and over with hundreds of salespeople at companies, small and large. Many of these items have been organized into the book that you are now holding and represent a straight-up way of selling. No gimmicks, just practical ways to improve your sales process.

There is a huge amount of thanks to give. To the sales managers that I worked for that showed me the way, to sellers that I was fortunate enough to work with and help along their way. And of course, thanks to our customers who made it all possible.

Always Challenge Yourself.

My comment to everyone, even if you are a first-day junior seller, is to challenge me. Never take my word for anything if you do not believe it. Test the idea, if it does not work, let me know and together we will improve.

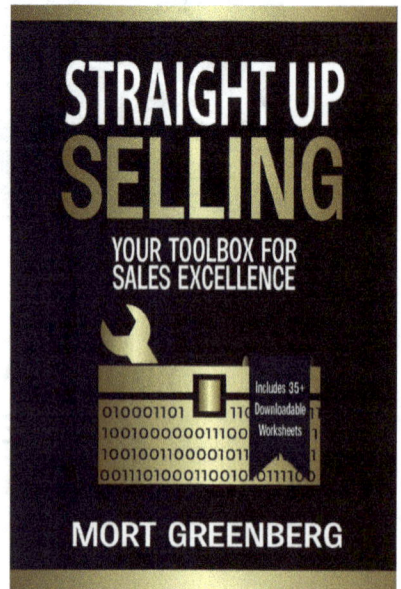

STRAIGHT UP SELLING

YOUR TOOLBOX FOR SALES EXCELLENCE

Includes 35+ Downloadable Worksheets

010001101 110
1001000000011100
1001001100001011
0011101000110010 01111

MORT GREENBERG

Since no one wants to just read about ideas without being able to quickly test them, there are a few worksheets in this book that you can start using from day 1. In fact, on the following pages, there are 35+ worksheets available with this book. By scanning the QR code to the right you can access all of them. Just add to the cart, for a no charge / free checkout. Whether you take some elements from this book and combine them with your current systems or just use the systems laid out here, you will find a way to improve your sales process and overall revenue generation.

Revenue vs. Sales

A key topic woven into this book is the difference between revenue and sales. Revenue is the outcome and end goal of selling. Where sales is the process we go through to generate revenue.

Always Build Upon Your Skills

There are six types of sales training companies can utilize for their sellers: Industry Training, Company Training, Product Training, General Sales Training, Leadership Training, and Sales Technique Training. What you will read on the pages ahead falls mainly into the last group, Sales Technique Training. Learning how to sell is a never-ending process. Everyone in every aspect of life sells at one time or another. Anyone that has been a seller, even if a new seller, knows firsthand that success in sales does not come easily. It requires hard work, dedication, and a willingness to continually improve and learn.

That's why you put in the time and effort to become better at selling. Whether you're just starting out in your career or you're a seasoned pro, there is always room to improve. Two of the biggest drivers that push sellers to get better and better are customer expectations and personal satisfaction.

Customer Expectations

Today's customers expect more from salespeople than ever before. They want knowledgeable, professional, and helpful salespeople who can provide them with valuable insights and solutions. Personal Satisfaction: As a salesperson, there is nothing quite like the feeling of closing a sale and knowing that you've helped someone solve a problem or meet a need. By putting in the time and effort to become a better seller, you'll be able to experience success more often. So, if you're serious about your career in sales, don't let complacency set in. Instead, commit to continuous learning, this will help you be the best seller possible. Your customers (and your bottom line) will thank you.

TABLE OF CONTENTS

CHAPTER 1

THE INTRODUCTION

"

You can't manage outcomes – you can only master actions. Sales is your system. Revenue is your reward.

"

Revenue vs. Sales:

Understanding the Difference

In any sales career, success hinges on a critical distinction: Revenue is the outcome. Sales is the process. Confusing the two is one of the most common — and costly — mistakes sellers make.

- **Revenue is the measurable result:** the dollars you bring into the business. It's the scorecard, the validation, the why behind all selling activity.

- **Sales is the journey:** the structured process of identifying prospects, creating value, overcoming objections, and converting conversations into commitments.

Key Insight:

You cannot manage revenue directly. You can only manage the sales activities that produce revenue.

Mindset Shift:

Top sellers focus not just on "closing deals" but on consistently executing a repeatable process that generates revenue predictably over time.

Why This Distinction Matters

- **If you focus only on sales:** You risk being busy without being productive. Meetings, calls, and emails feel satisfying, but may not drive outcomes.

- **If you focus only on revenue:** You become outcome-obsessed and reactive, chasing numbers without a clear, scalable system to achieve them.

Balance is everything.

You must measure both your *activity* and your *outcomes* – and continually fine-tune your process based on what the data tells you.

Setting Up Your Sales Process for Success

Think of your sales process like building a powerful engine. It needs the right structure, rhythm, and checkpoints to deliver consistent performance.

The Three Sales Process Time Horizons:

TIMEFRAME	FOCUS	GOAL
0–6 months	Build and Validate Your Sales Plan	Set a strong foundation: Know your product, your customers, and your value propositions.
7–12 months	Improve the Plan and Deals Sold	Upgrade the quality of deals: move to larger, more strategic accounts.
13–18+ months	Drive Scale and Repeat Business	Maximize referrals, upsells, and expansion into existing accounts.

Pro Tip: Most sellers underestimate how long it takes to truly hit stride. 18 months is a realistic timeline to become a consistent top performer – but you must sell from Day 1 while improving your system over time.

Build a Revenue-Generating Sales Process: Six Core Elements

STEP	WHAT YOU MUST DO	WHY IT MATTERS
1	Clarify Your Target Customers	Laser focus on where you win most often.
2	Design a Prospecting Plan	Control your pipeline by proactively reaching out.
3	Craft Value-Based Messaging	Talk about customer outcomes, not features.
4	Engage in High-Impact Meetings	Prepare, personalize, and guide the conversation.
5	Follow Up Relentlessly	Deals are rarely closed on first contact — persistence wins.
6	Track Metrics and Refine Weekly	Sell smarter every month by learning from your numbers.

Workshop Activities

1. Revenue vs. Sales Clarity Exercise

- Write down what you are doing daily that supports sales (the process).

- Write down how those activities are tied to revenue (the result).

- Identify any gaps — are you doing activities that feel "busy" but don't generate revenue?

2. The 18-Month Success Timeline

Create a personal timeline:

- **Month 1–6:** What skills or actions must you master?

- **Month 7–12:** What improvements must you make to your customer base or deal quality?

- **Month 13–18:** How will you expand and scale?

Example:

TIMEFRAME	ACTION PLAN
Months 1–6	Master cold prospecting and personalized outreach.
Months 7–12	Focus on closing $50k+ strategic accounts.
Months 13–18	Build referral systems inside current client accounts.

3. Sales Process Blueprint

Sketch your full sales cycle from first contact to close:

- How do you find leads?
- How do you qualify opportunities?
- How do you structure conversations?
- How do you follow up?
- How do you move from close to upsell?

The clearer you are about your process, the faster you can optimize it.

Tips to Supercharge Your Introduction Phase

- Be ruthlessly honest about where you waste time.
- Track your activities – not just results – for 30 days.

- Audit your meetings: Did you prepare customer insights or just show up?

- Use daily "5+5" discipline: Five new outbound contacts and five follow-ups — every single day.

- Celebrate small wins: They build momentum toward bigger closes.

Final Thought

"You don't rise to the level of your goals. You fall to the level of your systems." — James Clear, Atomic Habits

This book, and your commitment to upgrading your sales system, will make sure your floor keeps rising — until excellence becomes your default.

CHAPTER 2

SCALING OUTREACH TO BEAT YOUR REVENUE GOALS

> *Big goals aren't beaten with big talk —
> they're beaten with small daily wins,
> stacked one after another.*

Why Scaling Outreach is Non-Negotiable

If you want bigger revenue, you need a bigger top of funnel.

There is no magic shortcut:
More quality outreach = More meetings = More opportunities = More revenue.

Scaling outreach isn't about working harder — it's about working smarter and more systematically, making high-volume, high-quality touches every single day.

Task #1 — Fold A Sheet Of Paper Into Six Boxes

Take a blank sheet of paper and fold it into six equal sections. In each box, write:

LIST YOUR TOP CLIENT (Think what they like most a bout your deal)	**LIST YOUR TOP PROSPECT** (Think what they want to buy from you)	*This box will be filled in later in the book*
LIST 1 INDUSTRY ORG (You belong to or know about and should join)	**THINK ABOUT A MENTOR** (Who is someone that can be a mentor to you?)	*This box will be filled in later in the book*

TOP CLIENT: United Airlines.	**TOP PROSPECT:** Vans Sneakers	*Leave Blank (You will fill this later after initial meetings).*
VALUE: Seamless onboarding and reporting transparency.	**NEED:** Need to improve customer engagement digitally.	
New York Advertising Club	**MENTOR** Former manager at Excite.com.	*Leave Blank (You will fill this with new strategies learned during execution).*

This simple tool forces you to prioritize real people and communities you must nurture immediately.

Know Your Goals to Beat Your Goals (Individual or Team)

Setting goals isn't optional – it's foundational.

Individual Sellers:

- Know your annual revenue goal.

- Break it down into quarterly and monthly targets.

- Translate revenue goals into activity goals: How many meetings, proposals, and closed deals will it take?

Sales Teams:

- Create a transparent shared dashboard.

- Celebrate leading indicators (meetings booked, proposals sent), not just lagging indicators (revenue closed).

- Remember: Revenue is an outcome of repeatable behaviors.

Example:

If you close 20% of proposals, and each deal is worth $10,000, and you need $100,000 per quarter, you must generate 50 qualified meetings per quarter (approx. 4 per week).

Goal Tracking and Benchmarking

You can't improve what you don't measure.

Use these tools:

- **Quarterly Goal Tracker:** Compare your actual revenue vs. goal every single week.

- **Weekly Pipeline Updates:** Predict where you will finish the quarter by updating your pipeline every Friday.

- **Variance Alarms:** If you're behind plan, alert leadership early – not in the final weeks.

Visual Example: Quarterly Tracker

BOOKED v. GOAL
WEEKLY BOOKED BUSINESS TARGET = $XX

YOUR COMPANY NAME

202X CURRENT OUTLOOK

Data Source: Boostr Reports

	Q1	Q2	Q3	Q4	20XX YTD
200xx (000)					
Quarter	**Q1**	**Q2**	**Q3**	**Q4**	**20XX YTD**
Sales Goal	$ 4,000	$ 4,500	$ 5,000	$ 6,500	$ 20,000
Contracted Current Week	$ 3,786	$ 4,671	$ 4,800	$ 7,200	$ 20,467
Variance to Goal	$ (214)	$ 171	$ (200)	$ 730	$ 487
% to Goal	94.7%	103.8%	96.0%	111.2%	102.4%
Contracted Previous Week	$ 3,786	$ 4,671	$ 4,800	$ 6,600	$ 18,857
Variance vs. Previous Wk.	$ -	$ -	$ -	$ 630.0	$ 630.0
Pipeline	$ -	$ -	$ -	$ 2,310	$ 2,310
End of QTR Projected Finish	$ 3,786	$ 4,671	$ 4,800	$ 9,540	$ 22,797
% to Goal @ Projected Finish	94.7%	103.8%	96.0%	146.8%	114.0%
Year Prior Finish / Quarter	$ 3,400	$ 3,750	$ 3,821	$ 4,663	$ 15,634
$ Variance to Current Week	$ 386	$ 921	$ 979	$ 2,567	$ 4,853
% Variance to Current Wk.	11.4%	24.6%	25.6%	55.1%	31.0%

Legend:
- Contracted Current Week
- End of QTR Projected Finish
- Sales Goal

Chart values:
- $7,500
- $6,500 — $6,500
- $7,230
- $5,500
- $5,000
- $4,500 — $4,500
- $4,000
- $4,800
- $4,671
- $3,500 — $3,876
- $2,500
- $1,500
- $500
- $(500)

X-axis: 1 2 3 4

NOTES

Includes $50k +/- per month of programmatic. Does not include subscriptions, or corp licensing revenue

Focus on New Business
5 / 5 / 30

	1	2	3	4	5	6	
QX 202X (000)	Week Of >>>						
Week Starting	4-Jul	11-Jul	18-Jul	25-Jul	1-Aug	8-Aug	15
Sales Goal	$ 5,000	$ 5,000	$ 5,000	$ 5,000	$ 5,000	$ 5,000	$
Contracted	$ 2,449	$ 3,122	$ 3,400	$ 3,550	$ 3,600	$ 3,812	$
Variance to Goal	$ (2,551)	$ (1,878)	$ (1,600)	$ (1,450)	$ (1,400)	$ (1,188)	$
% to Goal	49.0%	62.4%	68.0%	71.0%	72.0%	76.2%	
W/W $Change (New Rev.)	$ -	$ 673.00	$ 278.00	$ 150.00	$ 50.00	$ 212.00	$
Pipe $ to Convert Each Wk.	$ -	$ -	$ -	$ -	$ -	$ -	$
End of Wk. Projected Finish	$ 2,449	$ 3,122	$ 3,400	$ 3,550	$ 3,600	$ 3,812	$
% to Goal @ Projected Finish	49.0%	62.4%	68.0%	71.0%	72.0%	76.2%	

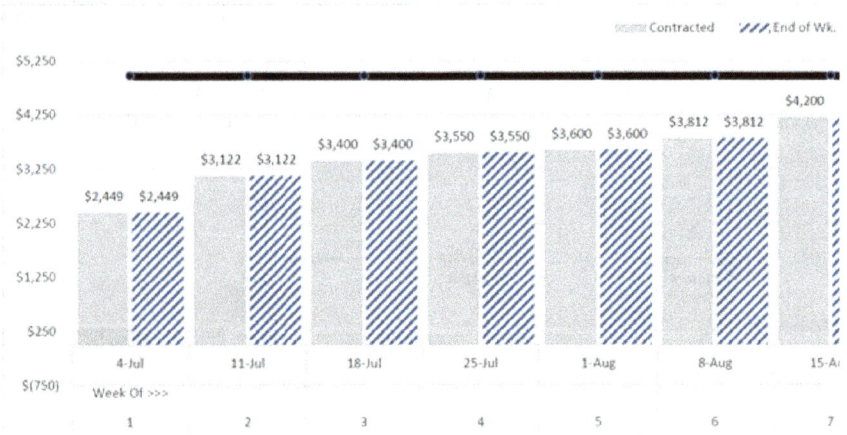

OUTLOOK TO FINISH

WEEKLY BOOKED BUSINESS TARGET = $X

7		8		9		10		11		12		13		NET $ in Q	Weekly Avg.
Aug		22-Aug		29-Aug		5-Sep		12-Sep		19-Sep		26-Sep			(000)
5,000	$	5,000	$	5,000	$	5,000	$	5,000	$	5,000	$	5,000			
4,200	$	4,622	$	4,800	$	4,800	$	4,800	$	4,800	$	4,800			
(800)	$	(378	$	(200)	$	(200)	$	(200)	$	(200)	$	(200)			
84.0%		92.4%		96.0%		96.0%		96.0%		96.0%		96.0%			
88.00	$	422.00	$	178.00	$	-	$	-	$	-	$	-	$	2,351.00	$ 195.92
-	$	-	$	150	$	150	$	-	$	-	$	-			
4,200	$	4,200	$	4,950	$	5,100	$	5,100	$	5,100	$	5,100			
84.0%		84.0%		99.0%		102.0%		102.0%		102.0%		102.0%			

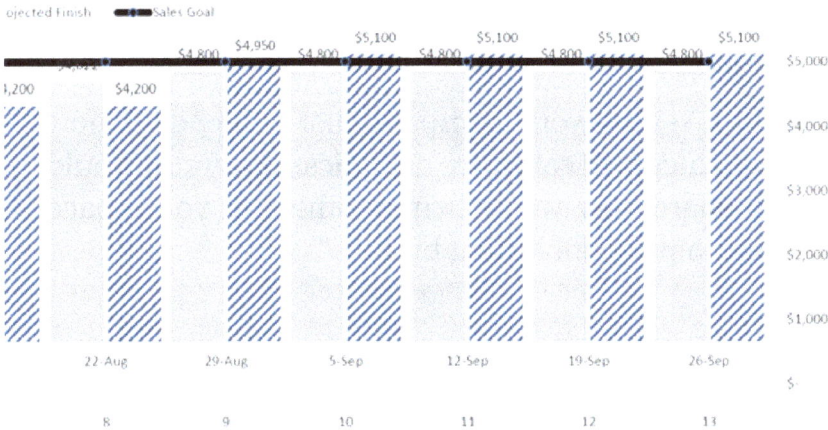

Scale Meeting Volume to Scale Revenue

Meetings are the currency of sales growth. No meetings = no new deals.

Scaling Secrets:

- It takes 3+ touches (email, call, LinkedIn) to get a prospect's attention.

- The average seller quits after 1–2 attempts. Top sellers make 5+ touches.

- Personalization wins. Don't just automate blasts – reference something specific about their company or role.

Example:

"Hi Alex – saw your company just launched a new SaaS product for healthcare analytics. Congrats! Would love to share how we've helped others in your space scale customer onboarding by 40%."

Minimum Daily Activity – The 5's

To scale consistently, apply the 5/5/30 rule:

DAILY ACTIVITY	WHAT TO DO	WHY IT WORKS
5 Outbounds	5 new prospect outreaches before lunch.	Keeps pipeline full.

DAILY ACTIVITY	WHAT TO DO	WHY IT WORKS
5 Follow-ups	5 follow-ups to previous prospects before dinner.	Ensures momentum on older leads.
30 Deals in Your Pipeline	30 Real pieces of business in your pipeline each month.	For every 10 deals you have 3 of those companies will be interested in your offering but only 1 will buy each month. 30 working deals means you will close 3+ deals each month.

Golden Rule:

You cannot go to bed until you hit your "5 + 5." It's the daily discipline that separates amateurs from pros.

Workshop Activities

1. Goal-Setting and Revenue Math Workshop

- Write down your annual revenue goal.
- Break it down by quarter and month.
- Estimate your average deal size and closing rate.
- Back-calculate: How many qualified meetings must you generate per week to stay on track?

2. Daily Outreach Tracker

Create a simple table:

DAY	NEW OUTBOUNDS (5)	FOLLOW-UPS (5)	NEW MEETINGS SET
Monday	✅	✅	2
Tuesday	✅	✅	1

Reward yourself for streaks of 5+ consecutive days.
If you can string together 21 days, it becomes a habit!

3. Pipeline Gap Early Warning Drill
Each Friday:

- Forecast where you will finish the quarter based on current deals + pipeline.

- Identify if you're trending ahead, on pace, or behind.

- If behind, list 3 proactive steps you will take immediately to recover.

Example Recovery Steps:

- Launch a targeted re-engagement email to past prospects.

- Block 2 hours Monday morning for pure prospecting.

- Offer a limited-time incentive to close hesitant deals.

Bonus Tips

- **Batch Your Prospecting:** Do 60 minutes in the morning when your mind is fresh.

- **Use Pre-Written Templates:** But personalize the opening 1–2 sentences every time.

- **Celebrate Outreach Wins:** Even small meetings booked deserve recognition — momentum builds.

- **Document Learning:** Every "no" is a data point. Why didn't they buy? Log it.

Final Thought

"You don't close sales. You open relationships that drive revenue."

Scaling outreach isn't just an action. It's a mindset of discipline, resilience, and curiosity.

By mastering the small daily behaviors that fuel massive revenue growth, you'll separate yourself from 90% of sellers who are simply "busy."

CHAPTER 3

HOW TO FIND THE BEST PROSPECTS AND STAND OUT

"

*Don't chase everyone. Find the few
who truly need you — and make
yourself unforgettable.*

Why Prospecting Is Your Secret Weapon

You can't sell to people who don't know you exist.

In today's hyper-competitive markets, prospecting isn't optional — it's your lifeline.

The best sellers are obsessed with prospecting:

- They don't wait for leads.

- They don't hope for referrals.

- They actively create opportunities.

If you want to consistently beat your number, prospecting must become a daily non-negotiable priority — not something you do when you have free time.

Prospecting Tips for B:B and B:C Sellers

For B2B (Business-to-Business) Sellers:

- Research industry events: Identify conferences, expos, webinars.

- Download exhibitor lists and attendee lists: Highlight companies that are not yet clients.

- Use tools like ZoomInfo, Apollo, and LinkedIn Sales Navigator to get key contacts.

For B2C (Business-to-Consumer) Sellers:

- Build your list through content marketing, lead magnets,

and social media advertising.

- Focus on where your audience spends their time: Instagram, TikTok, Facebook, YouTube.

- Collect emails ethically with valuable giveaways and follow up systematically.

Universal Prospecting Rule: Quality over quantity – but don't confuse caution with inactivity.

Example:
Instead of 500 cold emails, send 50 highly personalized, research-driven ones.

Plan Your Prospecting
Ahead of Time

Fail to plan = plan to fail – especially in prospecting.

Every Sunday Night:

- Build a list of 25 companies to target this week.

- Identify 2-3 key contacts at each company.

- Write quick notes: "Why is this company a fit?" and "What pain point can I solve?"

Every Morning:

- Research and personalize your outreach for that day's 5 targets.

- Find personal or company news to reference.

Every Afternoon:

- Execute 5+ follow-ups on emails sent last week.

Sample Prospecting Flow:

DAY	MORNING	AFTERNOON
Monday	Research and email 5 new prospects	Follow-up on last week's Monday outreach
Tuesday	Research and email 5 new prospects	Follow-up on last week's Tuesday outreach
...	...	...

Golden Rule:

Your calendar should always have prospecting blocks built in — and treated as seriously as client meetings.

Finding Your Best Prospects

How to find the right prospects (not just any prospects):

1. Conferences and Trade Shows:

- Get the speaker and sponsor lists.
- Target moderators and panelists – they are often influencers.

2. Industry Publications and Blogs:

- Read top industry news.
- Spot companies investing in new initiatives or expansion.

3. Webinars and Podcasts:

Look for companies that sponsor or guest-appear – they're active and growth-minded.

4. Social Listening:

Monitor LinkedIn and Twitter for executives posting about changes, hiring, or funding announcements.

5. Lead Enrichment Tools:

Use platforms like Hunter.io, Apollo, Clearbit, and Winmo to find emails and direct dials.

Account-Based Marketing (ABM)

What is ABM?

ABM is a focused strategy where sales and marketing work together to target specific high-value accounts with highly personalized messages and content.

The 4 Core Steps of ABM:

Step	Action	Example
1	Identify	Pick your top 50 highest potential companies.
2	Expand	Build multiple contacts inside each company.
3	Engage	Personalize emails, ads, and content to their challenges.
4	Advocate	Turn customers into references and upsell champions.

Modern ABM Tools:

- 6sense
- Demandbase
- Madison Logic
- Terminus

Example ABM Play:

- Personalized LinkedIn ad targeted to CFOs of 50 healthcare tech companies.
- Followed by customized emails highlighting how your solution reduces billing cycle times.

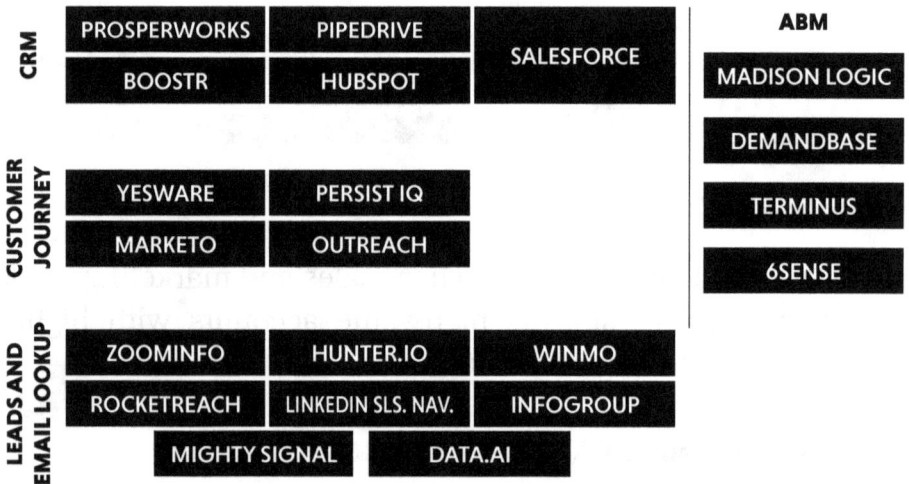

CRM	PROSPERWORKS	PIPEDRIVE	SALESFORCE	ABM
	BOOSTR	HUBSPOT		MADISON LOGIC
				DEMANDBASE
CUSTOMER JOURNEY	YESWARE	PERSIST IQ		TERMINUS
	MARKETO	OUTREACH		6SENSE
LEADS AND EMAIL LOOKUP	ZOOMINFO	HUNTER.IO	WINMO	
	ROCKETREACH	LINKEDIN SLS. NAV.	INFOGROUP	
	MIGHTY SIGNAL	DATA.AI		

Sales Emails:

3–5 Bullet Sentences Formula

Busy people don't read long emails. They scan.

Use this structure every time:

Bullet 1: Empathy or Personalization

- Congratulate them on recent news, funding, promotions.
- Reference a common connection or mutual interest.

Bullet 2: Value Proposition

- Who you are.
- What major problem you solve (keep it client-centric).

Bullet 3: Call to Action

- Ask for a short call, demo, or meeting.
- Be respectful, casual, but clear.

(Optional) Bullet 4+: Reinforcement

Add a link to a relevant case study or article if appropriate.

Example:

Hi Sarah,

- *Congrats on your recent expansion into new markets! Exciting times.*
- *I help companies like yours reduce customer churn by 23% with targeted onboarding campaigns.*
- *Would you be open to a 15-min call next week to discuss how we could help your growth?*
- *(Optional) Here's a quick case study from a similar client: [link]*

Thanks so much! – [Your Name]

Workshop Activities

1. Top Prospect List Building Sprint

- In 15 minutes, list 25 companies you want to target.
- For each company, write the top 1–2 decision-makers.
- Write one sentence about why each company is a fit for you.

Pro Tip:

Use LinkedIn filters: Company Size + Industry + Role Title.

2. Personalized Email Writing Challenge

- Choose 5 real prospects today.
- Write customized 3-bullet emails to each of them.
- Track open rates and responses.
- Adjust your style based on what works.

3. Account-Based Marketing Starter Plan

- Select your top 10 dream clients.
- Build a short profile for each: Industry, recent news, buying signals.
- Write 3 personalized ideas for how you can add value to each company.

Bonus Tips

- **Warm up cold leads:** Like, comment, or engage with their LinkedIn posts 1–2 weeks before emailing.

- **Use voice notes or short videos:** If appropriate, add a 20-second personalized video.

- **Always end emails with a question:** This increases response rates dramatically.

- **Automate but personalize:** Tools like Apollo or Outreach.io can help manage volume, but personalization wins meetings.

Final Thought

"Prospecting isn't something you do to get clients. It's something you do because you're a professional."

If you make prospecting mastery part of your identity – not just a task – you will never worry about missing your number again.

CHAPTER 4

SALES WRITING AND EMPLOYING EMPATHY

> *The words you choose and the empathy you show will open more doors than the hardest pitch ever could.*

Why Writing and Empathy are the Ultimate Sales Skills

In today's world of nonstop noise, your words must do more than just communicate — they must connect.

Great sales writing is never about you. It's about the customer, their challenges, and the value you can bring.

Empathy is the secret weapon behind powerful sales messages.

If your prospect feels like you understand them better than anyone else — they'll trust you to help solve their problems.

Big Idea:

"Sales isn't just talking — it's understanding, then communicating with clarity, respect, and relevance."

Task #2 — Boost Your Visibility!

Before people can buy from you, they must know you.

This task will help you build your personal visibility across channels where your prospects and customers already spend time.

Activity:

Fill out these prompts on a blank sheet or journal:

PROMPT	EXAMPLE
Top Client (What they like most about your deal)	United Airlines: "Fast onboarding and proactive support."

PROMPT	EXAMPLE
Top Prospect *(Why they should buy from you)*	Vans Sneakers: *"We can automate key customer touchpoints to boost retention."*
One Industry Organization	New York Advertising Club
One Mentor You Can Learn From	Former manager at Excite.com.
Your Social Media Accounts *(Posting or just watching?)*	LinkedIn active, Twitter inactive, Instagram watching only.
Important Trend to Start Posting About	New AI integrations.

Take a blank sheet of paper and fold it into six equal sections. In each box, write:

LIST YOUR TOP CLIENT (Think what they like most about your deal)	**LIST YOUR TOP PROSPECT** (Think what they want to buy from you)	**SOCIAL MEDIA ACCOUNTS** (Do you post regularly or just a voyer)
LIST 1 INDUSTRY ORG (You belong to or know about and should join)	**THINK ABOUT A MENTOR** (Who is someone that can be a mentor to you?)	**IMPORTANT TREND TO YOU** (Start posting and reposting on that topic)

Challenge Yourself:

Pick one platform (like LinkedIn) and commit to 1 post a week sharing insights, articles, or wins related to your industry.

Visibility fuels credibility. Credibility fuels opportunity.

Social Media – Become a "Smart" Content Creator

Social media isn't about showing off. It's about showing up.

Why Smart Posting Matters:

- It builds top-of-funnel awareness for you and your brand.
- It creates micro-moments of value that pull prospects toward you.
- It positions you as a trusted advisor, not just a seller.

What to Post:

- Educational content (how-to's, industry trends, frameworks).
- Celebrations of customer wins and milestones.
- Thoughtful commentary on new articles or industry news.
- Behind-the-scenes glimpses of your process, values, or learning journey.

Posting Best Practices:

Do	Don't
Post 2-3 times per week	Post only when desperate for leads
Check spelling, grammar	Post political or polarizing content
Add value before asking for anything	Only promote yourself
Stay consistent (even if only 1x/week)	Disappear for months at a time

Engagement = visibility.

Respond to comments, tag people when appropriate, and thank those who engage.

Sales Writing – Maximize "You" and "Your." Rarely Use "I."

Words matter. The wrong ones push people away. The right ones pull people closer.

Golden Writing Rule:

Always focus on the reader, not yourself.

You vs. I Writing Mindset:

- **Instead of:** "I would love to tell you about our amazing product."

- **Write:** "You'll discover faster ways to improve your team's performance by 20%."

Target:

- Use "You" and "Your" 5x more than "I".

- Challenge yourself to write emails without starting any sentence with "I."

Bullet Writing Framework:

- 5 bullets max per email.

- Each bullet = 1 clear thought, action, or benefit.

- No run-on sentences: 12 words or fewer per sentence when possible.

Example Upgrade:

Hi Alex,

- *Congrats on your team's recent Series B raise!*

- *You can use our platform to speed up your client onboarding by 30%.*

- *Would you like to see a 15-minute demo customized for your industry?*

Thanks again for considering this!
[Your Name]

Construction of Great Sales Notes

12 or less words in a sentence

Be specific

Use #'s and data when you can

Spell out acronyms

Avoid your industry's jargon

Attach a case study or one sheet

Phone Skills – The Phone is the Perfect Follow-Up Tool

The phone isn't dead. Cold calls might be tougher – but warm follow-up calls are gold.

When to Use the Phone:

- After 2 personalized emails have gone unanswered.

- After a prospect downloads a resource or attends a webinar.

- After a meeting, to confirm next steps.

Phone Call Flow:

1. Reference their context:

> *"Hi [Name], I'm following up on the note I sent about [topic]."*

2. Offer immediate value:

> *"I have a few ideas on how you can [solve a specific pain point]."*

3. Request a micro-commitment:

> *"Would 10 minutes next week make sense to walk through it?"*

Important:

- Never cold call blindly anymore – lead with context.

- Respect their time – if they sound rushed, offer to call back at a better time.

Example:

"Hi Taylor, saw you're expanding into telehealth services. Quick call to share some ways we helped a similar client launch faster. Would 10 minutes later this week work?"

Workshop Activities

1. You/Your Writing Challenge

- Rewrite 3 of your most recent sales emails.
- Count the number of times you use *"I"* – replace with *"You"* or *"Your."*
- Track reply rates over 2 weeks and measure the difference.

2. Social Media Starter Plan

- Choose your primary platform (e.g., LinkedIn).
- Post once a week for 30 days:
  - » **Week 1:** Introduce yourself and your mission to help customers.
  - » **Week 2:** Share a valuable resource or article.
  - » **Week 3:** Celebrate a client win or industry milestone.
  - » **Week 4:** Offer 3 tips related to your area of expertise.

3. Phone Follow-Up Sprint

- Pick 10 prospects who have gone dark.
- Call each one within 3 days.

- Keep voicemails short and value-focused: under 30 seconds.

Script:

"Hi [Name], it's [You] from [Company]. I'm following up on [email/topic]. I have 2 quick ideas that could [specific benefit]. Happy to send a quick summary email if easier. Thanks!"

Bonus Tips

- When writing sales notes or emails: Fewer words = clearer thinking = faster decisions.

- Use numbers and data points: *"Increase conversion by 28%"* is stronger than *"Improve results."*

- Always close with a question: Questions invite responses. Statements don't.

- Use preview text wisely: In email marketing, your subject line + preview text must together tell a compelling mini-story.

Final Thought

"People don't remember what you said. They remember how you made them feel."

Sales writing and empathy are two sides of the same coin. Master these skills, and you won't just get responses — you'll earn trust.

CHAPTER 5

PUT IN THE TIME BEFORE, DURING AND AFTER MEETINGS

"

Preparation isn't extra work — it's the quiet advantage that wins loud victories.

"

Why Meetings Are Your Revenue-Driving Events

Meetings are the battles where revenue is won or lost.

Each one represents a strategic opportunity to:

- Build trust
- Advance a sale
- Create value
- Differentiate yourself from the competition

Preparation before, engagement during, and follow-up after are the disciplines that separate high performers from average sellers.

Big Idea:

"How you prepare, run, and follow up after meetings determines your close rate more than any sales pitch ever could."

Create an Agenda with Your Customer

Before Every Meeting:

- Send a simple, clear agenda 24 hours in advance.
- Collaborate with your customer by asking:

    "Is there anything you'd like to add?"

MEETING
AGENDA

Meeting Leader	Date and Time of Meeting
<Enter Info>	<Enter Info>
Company/Division Meeting with	Meeting Location/Address or Zoom Link
<Enter Info>	<Enter Info>

<Enter Client Name> Attendees	<Enter Company Name> Attendees
<Enter Names> (Use ALT + Enter to add additional row(s))	<Enter Names> (Use ALT + Enter to add additional row(s))

Meeting Goals

1) Goal #1
2) Goal #2

Meeting Agenda Items

1) Item 1 (Use ALT + Enter to add additional row(s))
2) Item 2
3) Item 3
4) Item 4

Meeting Notes...

Sample Agenda Template:

SECTION	EXAMPLE
Section	[Your Name]
Date/Time	[Tuesday, 10:00 AM EST]
Attendees	[You + Customer Team]
Meeting Goals	[1) Understand needs; 2) Present solutions; 3) Next steps]
Key Agenda Items	[Intro, Customer Challenges, Solution Overview, Pricing Discussion]

Why it matters:

- Shows professionalism
- Creates structure and focus
- Puts customers at ease (people fear surprises)

Share Customer Brief:

Prep for People You Meet With

Before Meeting:

Prepare a Customer Brief summarizing:

CATEGORY	QUESTIONS TO ANSWER
Business Overview	What does the company do?
Current Situation	What market pressures are they facing?
Key Competitors	Who are they worried about?
Big Priorities	What's top-of-mind for leadership?
Current Solutions	What are they already using?

Place Your Logo here

CUSTOMER BRIEF

Date Prepared: **[date]**   *Customer:*   **[customer name]**

1. Client Overview

2. Situation Analysis
A. what is going on in the customer's marketplace

B. what is going on in the customer's marketplace)

C. What are the customer's....

D. What is putting pressure...

3. Needs Assumption
A. Address Current Understanding of Marketing Objectives, Tactics, and Strategies

B Address Unique Marketing Practices for Print, Digital, Social, and Email

Pro Tip: *Use a short 1-pager format. No walls of text — fast, skimmable info*

Share Customer History:

Prep for People You Meet With

[**Place Your Logo here**]

CUSTOMER BRIEF

Date Prepared: **[date]**   *Advertiser:* **[client name]**

Account Overview

1. How long have we worked with customer? Who has supported on our team?

2. What programs has client run with us in the past? What have spend levels been?

3. How have we serviced customer? How would customer rate us?

4. What important to the client?

5. Are we delivering what the client needs? How much variation between expectation and delivery?

Deepen your understanding by preparing a **Customer History** page:

Question	Answer
Past Projects	What did we deliver for them previously?
Past Challenges	What problems did they face?
Satisfaction Level	How happy were they with past work?
Unresolved Issues	Anything that needs fixing?
Relationship Status	Who were our allies and blockers?

Bonus:

Look at your CRM, email threads, and LinkedIn interactions. Understand the "emotional history" — was trust high, or was there tension?

Build Customer Map: Who

Supports You? Who Does Not?

Use a **Customer Relationship Map** to visually track influence:

CONTACT	TITLE	RELATIONSHIP	NOTES
Jane	CMO	Partner/Ally	Advocates for our solution.
Bob	CFO	Neutral	Needs stronger business case.
Lisa	VP Sales	Detractor	Prefers current vendor.

Relationship Status Legend:

● Partner/Ally   ● Neutral   ● Detractor

[**Place Your Logo here**]

CUSTOMER RELATIONSHIP MAP
(ENTER NAME OF CUSTOMER)

	5 PEOPLE WE NEED TO KNOW AND SPEND TIME WITH				
	CONTACT 1	CONTACT 1	CONTACT 1	CONTACT 1	CONTACT 1
RELATIONSHIP QUALIFICATION >> Enter #s in Rows 22-26 to Change Color	ANTI-SPONSOR	DETRACTOR	NEUTRAL	SUPPORTER	PARTNER ALLY
Name / Title					
Notes					
Activity(ies) they like					
Unique Facts About Them					
Have Spent Time with Outside of Office (Yes or No)					
Influencer or Decission Maker					
Ally of Our Competitor (Yes or No)					
Vocal about the value we bring to their company	2	4	6	6	8
Provides internal and competitive insights that strengthens our sales efforts	2	4	6	6	8
Alerts and guides us through political sensitiveness within their organization	2	4	6	6	8
Helps our company position a winning Value Proposition	2	4	4	6	8
Solicit our point of view beyond the specifics of our offering	2	4	6	6	8
RELATIONSHIP SCORE	10	20	26	30	40

Barometer Scale

0	2	4	6	8
NEVER	UNSURE	OCCASIONALLY	MOST OF TIME	ALWAYS

1 ≤ SCORE ≤ 15	ANTI-SPONSOR	= works againts you
16 ≤ SCORE ≤ 22	DETRACTOR	= skeptical
23 ≤ SCORE ≤ 29	NEUTRAL	= doesn't care either why
30 ≤ SCORE ≤ 36	SUPPORTER	= agrees with you
37 ≤ SCORE ≤ 40	PARTNER ALLY	= your biggest champion

At The Meeting: Get Customers to Ask Questions & Engage

Turn the meeting into a conversation, not a monologue.

Tactics to Drive Engagement:

- Start with 2 questions before you start presenting:

  "What's the most important outcome for you today?" "What are you hoping to solve in the next 90 days?"

- Build in checkpoints:

  "Does that align with what you're thinking?"

- Pause every 5–7 minutes to invite dialogue.

Remember:

People value meetings they feel actively involved in – not lectures they are trapped in.

Meeting Follow-up – Become the Best at Follow-Up

Immediately After the Meeting:

1. Send a summary email within 2–4 hours.
2. Thank them for their time.

3. Recap:

» Goal(s) of Meeting

» Attendees

» Notes / Main discussion points / Key Decisions

» Next steps (who owns what, by when)

Sample Follow-Up Structure:

SECTION	EXAMPLE
Thank You	*"Thank you for meeting with us today."*
Recap	"We discussed improving onboarding speed and customer retention."
Next Steps	"I'll send a proposal draft by Friday; you'll provide feedback by next Tuesday."
Follow-Up Meeting	"Let's reconvene next Thursday to finalize."

Note-Taking –
Brings Value to Others

During Meeting:

- Take written notes – do not type loudly on a laptop unless agreed.

- Capture:

  - Key questions they asked

  - Pain points they mentioned

  - Buying signals (e.g., "We need this solved by Q3.")

Why it Matters:

- Shows respect
- Builds credibility
- Protects you from memory gaps
- Allows fast and accurate follow-up

Bonus Tip:
Link notes to LinkedIn profiles or CRM for instant context next time.

Create a Project Tracker – Graphical or Linear

DELIVERABLE, DATES, AND MESSAGES					STORY		GTM
Issues	Solutions	Dates	Messages				
					<Action Items>		
							Innovation and Accountability (Continue Improvement)

NAME OF PROJECT + (OWNER)

LAUNCH TRACKER
AND TIMELINE

				Week of >>													
Item/Milestone	Owner	% Done	Target Date	Jan	Feb	Mar	Apr	May	Jun	Jul	Aug	Sep	Oct	Nov	Des		Status/Next Steps

After multiple meetings:

Use a simple Project Tracker to visually organize next steps.

ITEM	OWNER	STATUS	DUE DATE	NOTES
Proposal Draft	You	In Progress	Friday	Include retention case studies
Budget Approval	Client CFO	Pending	Next Tuesday	May require escalation
Contract Signature	Legal Teams	Pending	End of Month	Redlines expected

Why Use a Tracker:

In complex deals, buyers appreciate sellers who stay organized – it reduces perceived risk and friction.

Workshop Activities

1. Pre-Meeting Planning Sprint

- Pick your next customer meeting.
- Build a 1-page Customer Brief.
- Build a 1-page Customer History.
- Create a 6-point agenda to send 24 hours prior.

2. Relationship Mapping Exercise

For a key client account:

- List the top 5 stakeholders.
- Assign Relationship Status (Ally, Neutral, Detractor).
- Write 1 action step for each to strengthen or win them over.

3. Meeting Recap and Tracker Template

- After your next two meetings, send follow-up summaries using the Recap Formula.
- Build a simple Tracker in Google Sheets or Excel to manage outstanding tasks.

Pro Tip:
Track both internal and customer-side action items. Be the project quarterback.

Bonus Tips

- Always confirm next meeting date before leaving the room or Zoom.

- Involve multiple people on the customer side early – don't rely on just one champion.

- Ask permission to take notes – it subtly signals that what they say matters.

- Send visual trackers in updates – buyers love seeing project momentum at a glance.

Final Thought

"Amateurs wing meetings. Professionals win meetings by owning every stage: before, during, and after."

Meetings are not just touchpoints. They are the bridges that carry your prospect from interest to action. Master meetings – and you will master revenue.

CHAPTER 6

"THE NINE TOOL" TO INFORM YOUR SALES PROCESS

"

The seller who knows the customer better than anyone else wins more deals, earns more trust, and stays in the game longer.

"

Why "The Nine Tool"

Will Elevate Your Sales Game

Sales isn't just about pushing products — it's about **building systems that inform and guide better selling**.

The Nine Tool is your playbook for driving continuous improvement by:

- Understanding your customers deeply

- Spotting opportunities before competitors

- Building credibility internally and externally

Big Idea:

"Innovation in sales starts with better intelligence, not bigger discounts."

The best sellers don't just sell — they **study, synthesize**, and **strategize**.

Remember... Customers Like

Innovation & Improvement

Today's Customer Wants:

- New ideas they haven't thought of

- Improvements that make their life easier

- Partners who show proactive thinking

How You Win:

- Consistently bring them new perspectives.
- Solve problems before they fully articulate them.
- Deliver both strategic and practical innovation.

Pro Tip:

Your role is not just to "meet needs." Your role is to "expand possibilities."

First, Find Out What Others Depend on You For!

EVERYONE	1. Create Culture
	2. Source, Screen, Hire and Onboard
	3. Train/ Mentor/ Coach

SALES MANAGEMENT	1. Set Category/ Regional Coverage
	2. Define Customer Types and Prospects
	3. Find/ Eliminate Channel Conflict

SELLERS	1. Qualify Prospects
	2. Outreach and Follow-Up
	3. Be Specific In What to Sell

MARKETING	1. Develop GTM and Content Marketing Plan
	2. Create USP/ Value Proposition
	3. Create Sales Collateral

HR/ FINANCE	1. Build Sales Compensation Plan
	2. Build Sales Process and CRM Tools Suite
	3. Run and Forecast Sales

Internally:

- What does your team rely on you to deliver?
- Where are you seen as the expert?

Externally:

- What do your customers count on you for?
- What would they miss if you weren't their partner?

Activity:

Write down the top 3 strengths that people inside and outside your company associate with you.

Example:

Internal Dependency	External Dependency
Clear communication to management	Creative solutions to speed time-to-value
Reliable sales forecasts	Transparent pricing breakdowns
Cross-team coordination	Smooth project handovers

Conduct Internal and External Interviews

Don't guess. Ask.

Internal Interviews:

- Talk to Sales, Marketing, Product, and Customer Success teams.

- Ask:

  "What do you think we do best for customers?"

  "Where do you think we lose deals?"

External Interviews:

- Talk to active customers, churned customers, and lost prospects.

- Ask:

  "Why did you choose us?"

  "What could we have done better?"

Golden Insight:

Former customers often give you the most honest and actionable feedback.

[YOUR LOGO HERE]   **SELLER AND CUSTOMER QUESTIONS**

Positives/What Sellers Like at Our Company		

Issues/What Sellers do NOT Like at Our Company		

What Clients Like About Our Company		

What Clients do NOT Like About Our Company		

Chart Out the Buyer Experience

BUYER UTILITY

Uncovering blocks to buyer utility: Identity biggest problem areas/blocks	* In which stage are the biggest blocks to customer productivity? * In which stage are the biggest blocks to simplicity? * In which stage are the biggest blocks to convenience? * In which stage are the biggest blocks to reducing risks? * In which stage are the biggest blocks to fun and image?

The Six Stages of the Buyer Experience Cycle

	1 Purchase	2 Delivery	3 Use	4 Supplements	5 Maintenance	6 Upsell/Renew
What Stages Are Working Well						
What Stages Have Problems						

How long does it take to hear back from a seller or CSM? Are proposals and IOs turned around quickly? DO sellers entertain customers prior to sale? Once bought how do you follow-up, invoice on time?	How long does it take to go live? How difficult is it to work with rep and senior team? Do buyers have to reports themselves? If yes, how costly and difficult is this for buyer?	Does the product require training or expert assistance? How effective are the product's features and functions? Does the product or service deliver far more targetting or options than required by the average advertiser?	Do you need other vendors to make this product work? If so, how costly are they?	How easy to maintain deal, and upgrade the buy? How costly is c a m p a i g n maintenance?	What happens when campaign ends? How easy is it to wrap up and then move to renewal?

Map the Full Buyer Journey:

Stage	Questions to Ask
Awareness	How do they first hear about us?
Evaluation	What factors matter most when choosing a vendor?
Purchase	What made them say yes (or no)?
Post-Sale	Are we meeting expectations?

Visual Example:

Awareness -> Consideration -> Decision -> Implementation -> Renewal

Identify Breakpoints:

Where do most prospects drop off, stall, or slow down?

List Who is Not Buying You but Should

[YOUR LOGO HERE]   **NON CUSTOMERS**

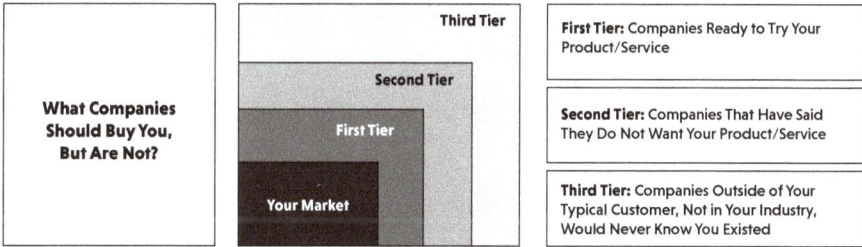

	Third Tier
What Companies Should Buy You, But Are Not?	Second Tier
	First Tier
	Your Market

First Tier: Companies Ready to Try Your Product/Service

Second Tier: Companies That Have Said They Do Not Want Your Product/Service

Third Tier: Companies Outside of Your Typical Customer, Not in Your Industry, Would Never Know You Existed

First Tier Targets	Second Tier Targets	Third Tier Targets
Target 1	Target 1	Target 1
Target 2	Target 2	Target 2
Target 3	Target 3	Target 3
Target 4	Target 4	Target 4
Target 5	Target 5	Target 5

Three Categories:

1. **First-Tier Targets:** Ready to buy – need slight nudge.

2. **Second-Tier Targets:** Familiar but skeptical – need education.

3. **Third-Tier Targets:** Unfamiliar with you – need awareness campaigns.

Exercise:

- List your Top 10 Dream Clients.
- Identify where they fall (Tier 1, 2, or 3).
- Plan 1 action per client to move them closer.

Example:

Company	Tier	Action
Vans Sneakers	Tier 1	Direct intro via LinkedIn + Case Study
Garmin Watches	Tier 2	Invite to exclusive webinar
Harley Davidson	Tier 3	Targeted LinkedIn ad campaign Motorcycles

Build a S.W.O.T.

[YOUR LOGO HERE]   S.W.O.T.

INTERNAL	STRENGTHS	WEAKNESS
	1)	1)
	2)	2)
	3)	3)
	4)	4)
	5)	5)

EXTERNAL	OPPORTUNITIES	THREATS
	1)	1)
	2)	2)
	3)	3)
	4)	4)
	5)	5)

- **Internal SWOT:** Strengths & Weaknesses of your current sales process.

- **External SWOT:** Opportunities & Threats in your customer's environment.

Example Grid:

Strengths	Weaknesses
Fast response time	Limited brand awareness
Deep industry expertise	Reactive vs proactive outreach

Opportunities	Threats
New regulations requiring your solution	Competitor launching cheaper alternative
Industry shift toward digitalization	Budget cuts in client industries

Pro Tip:
SWOT is not just a once-a-year exercise – revisit it quarterly.

FOUR ACTIONS FRAMEWORK

Use this Exercise to Challenge the Status Quo of Your Industry

List up to five factors for each (keep responses brief):

Reduce
Which factors should be *reduced below* industry's standard? (Think Costs)
1.
2.
3.
4.
5.

Raise
Which factors should be *reduced above* industry's standard? (Think Investment)
1.
2.
3.
4.
5.

Eliminate
Which factors the industry takes for granted to eliminate? (Think Costs)
1.
2.
3.
4.
5.

Create
Which factors should be created that industry has never offered (Think Investment)
1.
2.
3.
4.
5.

Summary of Differentiation

Internal Factors	Strength (S)	Weaknesses (W)
	1.	1.
	2.	2.
	3.	3.
	4.	4.
	5.	5.

What do you control internally?
Where do you need to partner externally?
What are the fastest wins?

External Factors

Opportunities (O)	S-O Strategies	W-O Strategies
1.	1.	1.
2.		
3.	2.	2.
4.		
5.	3.	3.

Threats (T)	S-T Strategies	W-T Strategies
1.	1.	1.
2.		
3.	2.	2.
4.		
5.	3.	3.

- **TOWS** is simply SWOT spelled backwards: Strengths, Weaknesses, Opportunities, and Threats.

- **TOWS matrix** is effective way to brainstorm specific strategies to address the result of SWOT investigation.

- **S-O** strategies pursue opportunities that match the company's strength.

- **W-O** strategies overcone weaknesses to pursue opportunities.

- **S-T** strategies identify ways you can use strengths to reduce vulnerability to external threats.

- **W-T** strategies establish a defensive plan to prevent weaknesses from making you susceptible to external threats.

Create an 8-Slide Internal Deck on How/What You Sell

INTERNAL MESSAGE
8 SLIDE INTERNAL NEW SELLER COMPANY EDUCATION

OVERVIEW	CUSTOMER
What you do?	How many types of customers do you have? What categories by type?

TYPE OF SALE	WHO IS SELLER?
Is this a complex sale or short term / relationship driven sale?	Direct sales, inside sales, indirect/3rd party sales

PRICE/FEE	ALTERNATIVES
What is the price or fee you will charge? What do competitors charge?	Who else is doing this? What are customers alternatives?

VALUE POINTS	TARGET CUSTOMERS
What are the differentiators vs. competitors?	What brand are you targetting?

Internal Enablement Deck Structure:

1. Our Ideal Customer Profile

2. What Problems We Solve

3. Our Unique Value Proposition

4. Key Case Studies

5. Competitive Differentiators

6. Objection Handling Playbook

7. Current Target Accounts

8. Pipeline Snapshot + Goals

Purpose:
Keep your entire internal team aligned and confident.

Create a 9-Slide External

Customer Presentation

EXTERNAL MESSAGING

9 SLIDE EXTERNAL SELLER TO CUSTOMER PRESENTATION

MARKET	PROBLEM YOU SOLVE
What part of advertising market are you creating value for? What are the key trends?	What problems do you have solutions for that talk to each client type?

PRODUCT/SERVICE	MARKET BENEFITS
What are your product and services? How do they work?	What are the benefits the market will derive from the product or service?

ALTERNATIVES	PROOF
What alternative options does the market have to your product? How are you better?	What proof evidence is there to substantiate your value proposition?

CUSTOMER BENEFITS	COSTS
List benefits for customer. How do you make the customers life better?	List costs for customers

VALUE GAINED
List value or ROI gained for customer

External Customer Deck Structure:

1. Introduction & Mission

2. Understanding Your Challenges

3. Industry Trends / Insights

4. How We Can Help

5. Our Solution Overview

6. Why Us (Differentiators)

7. Success Stories / Testimonials

8. Implementation Roadmap

9. Call-to-Action / Next Steps

Golden Rule:
Make the deck 70% about them, 30% about you.

Synthesize into a :10 and :30-Second Elevator Pitch

10-Second Pitch (Attention-Grabber):

"We help healthcare companies speed patient onboarding by 30% with smarter tech."

30-Second Pitch (Quick Story Arc):

"Healthcare companies struggle with onboarding delays that hurt patient satisfaction and revenue. Our platform automates onboarding tasks and communication, reducing delays by 30% in 90 days. Would you be open to seeing how it could help your team?"

Tip:
Always have both versions ready — conversations move fast.

10 Second Sales Pitch	30 Second Sales Pitch
Address what we do? The main job of our company is to... • Item 1 • Item 2 • Item 3	**Recent news and awards** Some highlights from the past few months... • Item 1 • Item 2 • Item 3
Address what makes us different? We are different because... • Item 1 • Item 2 • Item 3	**Address how customers can do X with us...** Do X through... • Item 1 • Item 2 • Item 3
Address how we're better? Other customers like what we offer... • Item 1 • Item 2 • Item 3	**What is new with you and your company?** Ask to get time on phone/ Zoom/ in Person to talk about... • Item 1 • Item 2 • Item 3

Create a Customer
Advisory Board (CAB)

What is a CAB?

- A small, curated group of trusted customers who give you direct feedback.

- A built-in source of market intelligence and product innovation ideas.

How to Build a CAB:

1. Select 5–10 top customers who represent different segments.

2. Meet virtually or in-person every 6 months.

3. Share roadmap updates; ask for feedback.

4. Recognize CAB members publicly – awards, LinkedIn shout-outs, VIP experiences.

Pro Tip:
CABs build loyalty and help you co-create future solutions with customers.

Workshop Activities

1. 9-Tool Mapping Sprint

- Sketch out a 1-page map listing:
- Your Top 3 strengths
- Top 3 customer pain points
- Buyer journey breakpoints
- 5 dream clients you're missing
- SWOT for your top product/service

2. Internal and External Deck Draft Challenge

- Create first drafts of:
- 8-slide internal deck for your sales team.
- 9-slide customer-facing presentation.

3. Elevator Pitch Practice

- Write your 10-second and 30-second pitches.

- Record yourself saying them.

- Adjust until they feel natural and compelling — not rehearsed.

Bonus Tips

- **Study competitors' decks** — learn what they're doing well (or poorly).

- **Update your SWOT every quarter** — the market changes faster than you think.

- **Build your CAB carefully** — include both friendly and challenging customers for real insights.

- **Never memorize your elevator pitch** — memorize the structure, then speak naturally.

Final Thought

"The best sellers are the best listeners — and the best architects of new opportunities."

The Nine Tool isn't just a framework — it's your system for staying customer-obsessed, evolving faster, and winning smarter.

CHAPTER 7

FORGING EXCEPTIONALISM

"

You don't rise to the level of your goals.
You fall to the level of your preparation
and discipline. Build both.

"

Why Exceptionalism is the Ultimate Competitive Advantage

In sales – and in life – the margin between good and great is razor thin. But those who cross that line? They become unforgettable.

Exceptionalism is not a one-time action.

It's a daily commitment to excellence, fueled by mindset, discipline, and resilience.

Big Idea:

"The battle for exceptional results is won in the daily habits no one sees."

Mindset & Muscle Memory

PLAN

TRAIN

VISUALIZE

VISUALIZE HOW YOU WILL MAKE CONTACT
VISUALIZE HOW YOU WILL FOLLOW-UP
VISUALIZE SENDING THE PROPOSAL
VISUALIZE GETTING TO AGREEMENT
VISUALIZE GETTING PAID!

Mindset:

- View obstacles as opportunities to strengthen your skills.

- Treat every rejection not as personal failure, but as valuable feedback.

Muscle Memory:

- Repeat best practices daily until they become automatic.

- Exceptional sellers do not "rise to the occasion" — they fall back on their training.

Example:

- **Before every call:** Review the agenda, customer history, and desired outcomes.

- **After every meeting:** Follow-up sent within 4 hours — without needing reminders.

Pro Tip:

Rituals build resilience. Build a pre-call checklist, a pre-meeting ritual, and a weekly self-review.

Your Thoughts and Words Matter

Self-Talk Shapes Outcomes:

- If you think you're behind, you act with hesitation.

- If you think you are valuable, you engage with confidence.

Outward Language Matters Too:

- **Never say:** *"I just wanted to follow up..."* — It sounds apologetic.

- **Instead say:** *"I'm reaching out to move forward on X"* — It sounds confident.

Internal Language Upgrade:

Weak Language	Strong Language
"I'll try"	*"I will"*
"Hopefully"	*"Confidently"*
"If it's OK"	*"Let's move forward"*

Pro Tip:
Your customers are subconsciously influenced by your tone, certainty, and positivity.

Avoid Anger and Keep Your Ego in Check

Anger:

- Never, ever let frustration leak into emails, calls, or meetings.

- If emotions rise, pause before responding — *"slow is smooth, smooth is fast."*

Ego:

- Remember: The customer is the hero, you are the guide.
- Humility builds trust faster than bravado.

Golden Rules:

- Stay calm under pressure: It's a competitive advantage.
- Detach personal identity from deal outcomes: You win some, you learn from some.

Example:

If a customer criticizes your product, thank them for their honesty – and ask for specific feedback you can act on.

Failure – It is a Good System

Rethink Failure:

- Failure is not a verdict. It's a version update.
- Every "no" teaches you something about positioning, timing, or qualification.

Fail Forward Process:

1. Acknowledge the loss quickly (no denial).
2. Diagnose what went wrong (facts, not feelings).
3. Adjust your strategy (experiment smarter next time).

Example:

- Lost a deal because you focused too much on features instead of business impact?

- In future meetings, reframe your approach: *Problem -> Impact -> Solution -> Proof.*

Pro Tip:

Failure is simply data. The best sellers are the best data scientists of their own performance.

No Surprises

Golden Commandment:

Customers, teammates, and managers should never be blindsided.

How to Avoid Surprises:

- If a deal is slipping, raise the flag early.

- If you need help from internal teams, ask with plenty of lead time.

- Confirm action items immediately after meetings.

Example:

"After today's meeting, here's the quick recap: Next steps are [X], by [date]. Please let me know if I missed anything!"

Pro Tip:
Predictability builds trust. Trust closes deals.

Own The Effort!

The Only Thing You Fully Control:

- Your preparation
- Your attitude
- Your effort

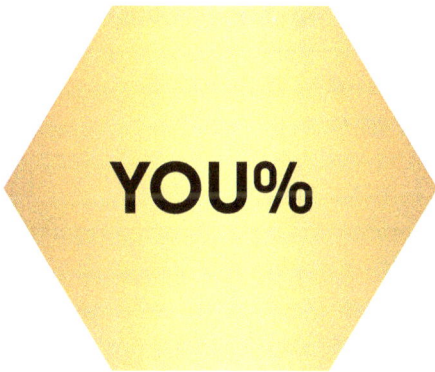

YOU%

THEM%

WHAT % EFFORT SHOULD YOU PUT IN? SHOULD ANOTHER PUT IN?

Keys to Owning the Effort:

- Show up early.
- Out-research everyone else.
- Out-follow-up everyone else.
- Out-improve yourself week over week.

Lead by Example

YOU 100%

THEM 0%

PUT IN THE WORK AND HAVE AN ANYTHING IS POSSIBLE, POSITIVE MINDSET

Ownership Mindset Example:

Mediocre Seller	Exceptional Seller
"No one gave me leads."	*"I built my own pipeline."*
"Marketing didn't support me."	*"I created my own customer stories."*
"It's not my fault."	*"It's my responsibility."*

Workshop Activities

1. Mindset Upgrade Exercise

- Write down three limiting beliefs you've had about sales or performance.
- Rewrite each one into an empowering belief.

Example:
From: *"Selling is pushy."*
To: *"Selling is helping people solve important problems."*

2. Daily Ritual Design

- Design a 10-minute **"Pre-Sales Ritual"** you do every morning:
  - » Review today's meetings.
  - » Visualize best-case outcomes.
  - » Write one thing you're grateful for.

- Design a 10-minute **"Post-Sales Ritual"** you do every evening:
  - » Review wins and learnings.
  - » Plan tomorrow's top 3 priorities.

3. Failure Feedback Loop

After every lost deal for the next 60 days, conduct a quick 3-question self-review:

- What went well?
- What would I change next time?
- What signals did I miss early?

Pro Tip:
Make this a non-negotiable habit, not a punishment.

Bonus Tips

- Respond – never react.
- Celebrate effort, not just outcomes.
- Journal lessons weekly. (Growth compounds through reflection.)
- Have an "ego check" partner – someone who tells you the truth, not what you want to hear.

Final Thought

"Exceptionalism isn't an event — it's a decision made every day, in every small action."

Master your mindset. Master your craft. Exceptionalism is earned by the way you show up when no one is watching.

CHAPTER 8

MAXIMIZING COMMUNICATION – LLTQC

"

In every conversation, the best communicator isn't the one who speaks first — it's the one who listens best.

"

Why LLTQC is the Salesperson's Secret Advantage

Top performers don't just *"talk better"* — they communicate better. And real communication isn't about speaking first. It's about reading, listening, thinking, and responding with purpose.

The LLTQC Framework — *Look, Listen, Think, Question, Communicate* — is your system for mastering the flow of customer conversations.

> **Big Idea:**
> *"Great salespeople are not the best talkers — they are the best interpreters of reality."*

LLTQC: The 5 Elements of Communication Mastery

LOOK – What are the Non-Verbal Signals?

80% of communication is non-verbal.

Reading body language, facial expressions, and energy levels can tell you more than words ever will.

Key Visual Cues to Watch For:

Positive Signals	Negative Signals
Leaning in	Crossed arms

Positive Signals	Negative Signals
Nodding	Avoiding eye contact
Smiling	Fidgeting or glancing at phone
Relaxed posture	Tense jaw, clenched hands

Examples of Visual Inconsistencies:

- Customer says, *"Sounds good"* but frowns – hidden objection.
- Customer says, *"We're happy with our vendor"* but shifts uncomfortably – possible dissatisfaction.

Pro Tip:

Always trust behavior more than words. If they don't match, dig deeper politely.

LISTEN – Active Listening

Active Listening =
Focused Attention + Purposeful Response.

Signs You Are Truly Listening:

- You aren't mentally rehearsing your next pitch.
- You can paraphrase what they just said – accurately.
- You ask clarifying questions instead of moving immediately to solutions.

Active Listening Techniques:

- Echo: Repeat key points in their words (*"So what I'm hearing is..."*).
- Label: Name emotions (*"It sounds like you're frustrated with the current process..."*).
- Silence: Let silence do the work – don't rush to fill gaps.

> **Pro Tip:**
> Listening isn't about waiting your turn to talk. It's about making the customer feel heard, seen, and respected.

THINK – Bring Together What You Are Seeing and Hearing

Think before you respond.

After you LOOK and LISTEN:

- **Analyze:** Are there gaps between what they say and how they behave?
- **Prioritize:** Which points seem most emotionally charged or urgent?
- **Strategize:** Which needs can you address now, and which need a bigger conversation later?

> **Example Thought Process:**
> - **Visual cue:** Customer looks uneasy when discussing pricing.

- **Listening cue:** They keep mentioning "budgets tightening."
- **Strategic thought:** Focus next on ROI, not just product features.

Pro Tip:
Great sellers are like detectives – picking up tiny signals to build the real story behind the buyer's words.

QUESTION – Focus on What You Ask

Questions are your most powerful tool –
if used wisely.

Great Sales Questions:

- Are open-ended (*"How are you currently handling X?"*)
- Dig beneath surface issues (*"What happens if that problem isn't solved?"*)
- Explore emotion, not just logic (*"How does this impact your team personally?"*)

Question Pitfalls to Avoid:

- Yes/No traps (*"Are you happy with your current vendor?"* -> Easy brush-off.)
- Rapid-fire interrogation (feels like an interrogation, not a conversation).
- Rhetorical questions (they close off dialogue).

Best Practice:

Goal	Example Question
Understand pain	*"What's your biggest challenge with your current system?"*
Clarify urgency	*"How soon do you need this solution in place?"*
Explore personal impact	*"How does this affect your day-to-day workflow?"*

COMMUNICATE – Once You Have Your Input, Communicate

Now – and only now – do you communicate.

Effective Communication Steps:

1. Reflect back what you heard:
   "It sounds like your key priorities are X, Y, and Z."

2. Offer relevant solutions:
   "Here's how we could help you address X immediately, and work toward Y and Z over the next 90 days."

3. Confirm agreement:
   "Does that align with what you were hoping for?"

Remember:

- Speak **with** the customer, not **at** the customer.

- Tie every recommendation back to something they said or showed.

- End with clear next steps.

Workshop Activities

1. Non-Verbal Cue Drill

- Watch a short YouTube interview muted.

- Write down all body language cues you notice.

- Then rewatch with sound – how accurate were your guesses?

2. Active Listening Roleplay

- Partner with a peer.

- One person plays "customer," one "seller."

- Practice:
  » Echoing key phrases.
  » Labeling emotions.
  » Staying silent after responses.
  » Swap roles after 10 minutes.

3. Question Library Creation

- Create a personal library of 15 powerful sales questions:
  » 5 pain-based questions
  » 5 urgency-focused questions
  » 5 emotional/impact questions

- Practice using 1–2 questions from each category in your next 5 sales calls.

▌ Bonus Tips

- **Practice micro-pauses** before answering – it shows you are thinking, not reacting.
- **Always confirm understanding** before pitching.
- **Record key meetings** (with permission) to review communication strengths and gaps.
- **Write a 1-line summary** after each meeting of what the customer's true priority is – train your brain to think in terms of their needs first.

Final Thought

"The greatest gift you can give someone is the feeling that they've been fully understood."

Master LLTQC, and you won't just improve your sales – you'll build deeper trust, stronger relationships, and longer-lasting customer loyalty.

CHAPTER 9

SEVEN-STEP PR TO GAIN INBOUND LEADS AND DRIVE REVENUE

"

The best sales strategy starts long before the first call – it starts by making sure the world already knows your story.

"

Why PR is a Critical Revenue Driver

Most sellers think of PR as something marketing handles.

Top sellers understand that smart PR is a pipeline machine — creating awareness, credibility, and inbound leads before a sales conversation ever starts.

Modern PR = Public Relations + Press Releases + Personal Branding + Content Marketing.

Big Idea:
"Good sellers chase leads. Great sellers attract opportunities."

Step 1: PR = Public Relations and Press Releases — Do Both!

Public Relations

- Building long-term relationships with media, influencers, and industry thought leaders.

- Becoming a known voice in your space.

Press Releases

- Official company announcements (new product, big client, funding round, award).

- Gives credibility, SEO impact, and helps fill your top of funnel.

Modern PR Pro Tip:

Combine formal press releases with informal PR outreach (social posts, DMs, direct pitches) to multiply visibility.

Example:

New product launch -> Formal press release + Personal outreach to 15 reporters on LinkedIn.

Step 2: Highlight Your Company's Basic Info

Before doing PR, get your foundational messaging tight.

Category	What to Define
Mission	Why does your company exist?
Value Proposition	What problem do you solve best?
Ideal Customer	Who are you built to serve?
Key Differentiators	What makes you better or different?

One-Pager Tip:

Create a fast "PR Cheat Sheet" with these basics for any media pitch or journalist request.

BASIC INFO	DETAIL	COMPANY FOUNDATION	DETAIL	PR AND MESSAGING	DETAIL
Company Name		Company Mission		Key Messages for Core Audiences	
Company Spelling		Why Work with FitAd		Key Message for Investors	
Company URL		Company Vision		3rd Party References	
Company Tag Line		What do we do?		What is our product	
When did company Launch		What do we NOT do?		What is unique about us?	

Sample Statement:

"[Company] helps [Customer Type] achieve [Big Outcome] by [Unique Solution]."

Step 3: Map Out Your Content Marketing Program Steps

Content Marketing Fuels PR:

Content Type	Goal
Blog Posts	Establish expertise
Case Studies	Showcase results
Webinars	Build authority
Podcasts	Humanize leadership
LinkedIn Posts	Boost visibility and engagement

Place Your
Logo here

CONTENT MARKETING OVERVIEW
Fall 202X

CONTENT MARKETING AND FACE TO FACE INTERACTION PLAN

Items (In Priority Order, Focus On Low Cost, But Effective Item First)	KPI	Daily or Weekly	2x / Month	1x / Month	Quarterly
SALES DRIVEN					
Client Meetings - General		<< x >>			
Client Meetings - Breakfast / Lunch & Learns		<< x >>			
Happy Hours & Dinners - 10-30 PPL				<< x >>	
Conferences / Events - 2 Tickets to Attend					<< x >>
MARKETING DRIVEN					
PR / Reporter Outreach / Press Release				<< x >>	
Research Reports - Internal Data					<< x >>
Holiday Cards & Gifts					<< x >>
Newsletters to Customers & Prospects			<< x >>		
Questionnaires to Customers & Prospects					<< x >>
White Papers on Key Topics					<< x >>
Research Reports - Third Party Driven					<< x >>
Conferences / Events - Sponsorship					<< x >>
SALES OUTBOND COMM. FLOW					
Intro Note		<< x >>			
Follow Up #1		<< x >>			
Follow Up #2			<< x >>		
Phone Call #1				<< x >>	

BUYER JOURNEY

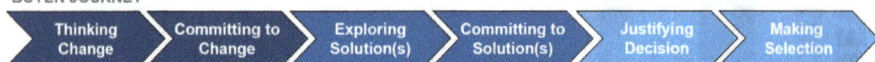

| Thinking Change | Committing to Change | Exploring Solution(s) | Committing to Solution(s) | Justifying Decision | Making Selection |

SELLER JOURNEY

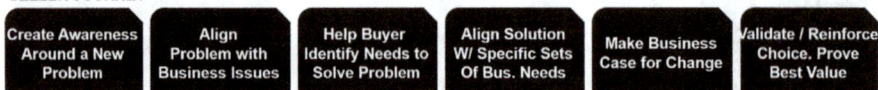

| Create Awareness Around a New Problem | Align Problem with Business Issues | Help Buyer Identify Needs to Solve Problem | Align Solution W/ Specific Sets Of Bus. Needs | Make Business Case for Change | Validate / Reinforce Choice. Prove Best Value |

SELLER DELIVERY OF CONTENT / PROOF TO BUYER

| Research / White Papers | Webcasts / Events | Assessment Tools | Case Studies / Testimonials | ROI Analysis Tools | Feature Comparison |

Content Planning Tips:

- Align your content to customer pain points and industry trends.
- Publish consistently — even one piece a week compounds fast.

Example Campaign:

March: Publish 2 blog posts on emerging industry trends.

April: Launch a customer case study + PR announcement.

May: Host a panel discussion webinar + repurpose clips for social.

Step 4: Map Out Your Public Relations and Press Release Efforts

PR PLAN
Fall 202X

Place Your Logo here

	Week 1	Week 2	Week 3	Week 4	Week 5	Week 6	Week 7	Week 8	Week 9	Week 10	Week 11	Week 12
PRESS RELEASE		PRESS RELEASE #1				PRESS RELEASE #2				PRESS RELEASE #3		
	Kick-Off Call	Finalize media target list	Draft FIRST formal press release	Pitch announcement to business reporters	Repeat Week #4 Until Enough Outlets Cover the Story	Draft SECOND press release	Pitch SECOND press release to business reporters	Repeat Week #7 Until Enough Outlets Cover the Story	Draft THIRD press release	Pitch THIRD press release to business reporters	Repeat Week #10 Until Enough Outlets Cover the Story	Develop press release calendar for next three months
	Write Messaging Plan	Draft PR plan	Pitch announcement exclusive	Pitch announcement to tech reporters		Finalize SECOND press release	Pitch announcement to tech reporters		Finalize SECOND press release	Pitch announcement to tech reporters		
	Audit background materials/media kits	Finalize PR plan	Create speaking calendar/matrix	Pitch announcement to ad/marketing reporters		Draft Thought leadership editorial calendar	Pitch announcement to ad/marketing reporters		Draft Thought leadership editorial calendar	Pitch announcement to ad/marketing reporters		
	v1 list of media outlets to target	Determine pitching strategy for FIRST announcement (exclusive?)	Finalize additional press targets for announcement release	Pitch announcement to general interest, as appropriate		Finalize speaking calendar/matrix	Pitch announcement to general interest as appropriate		Finalize speaking calendar/matrix	Pitch announcement to general interest as appropriate		
			Status update meeting	Pitch announcement to regional reporters		Pitch speaking opps	Pitch announcement to regional reporters		Pitch speaking opps	Pitch announcement to regional reporters		
			Create interview schedule matrix	Status update meeting		Status update meeting	Status update meeting		Status update meeting	Status update meeting		
			Coordinate exclusive interview	Coordinate interviews			Coordinate interviews			Coordinate interviews		

Press Release Calendar Example:

Month	Press Activity
March	Announce new product feature
May	Announce major customer win
August	Executive op-ed on future of industry
October	Host media roundtable at industry event

Key Tip:

PR isn't just reactive – it's proactive storytelling

Press Release Essentials:

- Clear, non-jargony headlines

- Lead with why it matters

- Include quotes from customers and leadership

- Offer a clear call-to-action or next step

Step 5: Develop Your Primary, Secondary and Tertiary Messages by Audience

MESSAGING
Fall 202X

Place Your
Logo here

	Why Company Matters?	Primary Message	Secondary Message	Tertiary Message
Everyone				
Audience 1				
Audience 2				
Audience 3				
Audience 4				
Investors				

Different audiences care about different things

AUDIENCE	PRIMARY MESSAGE	SECONDARY	TERTIARY
Customers	How you solve their problem better	Proof through case studies	Cost/value ROI
Investors	Growth potential and traction	Scalability of model	Management team strength
Media	Newsworthiness	Industry impact	Story's human interest angle

Example:

Same product announcement -> 3 different headlines for customers, investors, and journalists.

Pro Tip:

Never send a "one-size-fits-all" pitch — align to what each audience cares about most.

Step 6: List Out Media Outlets to Contact by Key Category

Three Types of Media Wins:

- **Earned Media:** Stories you get featured in (no payment).

- **Owned Media:** Content you publish yourself (blogs, LinkedIn).

- **Paid Media:** Sponsored posts or advertorials (use sparingly).

Build a simple Media Target List:

Category	Outlet Examples
Industry-Specific	Defense News, TechCrunch, Healthcare IT News
Business General	Forbes, Bloomberg, Business Insider
Regional	Your city's top business journals
Vertical Trades	Engineering Today, Retail Dive

Step 7: List Names of Reporters and Contact Info by Media Outlet

Reporter Target List Template:

OUTLET	REPORTER	BEAT	CONTACT INFO
TechCrunch	Jane Doe	SaaS Startups	jane.doe@techcrunch.com
Defense News	John Smith	Aerospace and Defense	jsmith@defensenews.com

Key Tip:

- Follow reporters on LinkedIn and Twitter before pitching.
- Comment meaningfully on their articles – build relationships first.

Golden Rule:

Help reporters win (great stories) and they will help you win (visibility).

Bonus Step: Develop a List of Events to Attend & Panels to Speak On

Speaking is PR Rocket Fuel

Event	Opportunity
Major Trade Shows	Speaking panels, sponsorships
Industry Webinars	Guest appearances
Local Chamber Event	Workshops or keynotes

Steps to Get on Panels:

- Apply early – most panels are booked 6–9 months in advance.
- Highlight your expertise, not just your company.
- Volunteer to moderate if speaking slots are filled.

Once Your Story Is Locked, Use "PR" To Promote It

Maximize Every PR Win:

- Post it on LinkedIn and tag people/companies mentioned.
- Repurpose it into a blog post.
- Include it in your email signature for 60 days.

- Share it internally to boost employee morale.
- Re-share it again 30–60 days later – audiences forget fast.

Golden PR Mindset:
"Don't just earn attention – amplify it."

Workshop Activities

1. PR Story Sprint

- Write your company's "One-Liner":
  [We help X solve Y by Z.]
- Write a 1-paragraph Press Release Summary:
  What would your next big headline be?

2. Media Target List Challenge

- Build a 10-contact media list:
  - » 5 industry-specific outlets
  - » 3 general business outlets
  - » 2 local/regional media
- Include reporter names and emails if possible.

3. Speaking Opportunity Research

- Find 5 events where your company could either:
  - » Submit a speaker.
  - » Apply to be on a panel.
  - » Host a booth + get media coverage.
- Plan to pitch at least 2 within the next 60 days.

Bonus Tips

- PR is about consistency, not bursts.

- **Start small if needed** – regional wins compound into national ones.

- **Think multimedia** – podcasts, videos, and panels count as PR too.

- **Always think like a journalist:** "Why would anyone outside our company care?"

Final Thought

"In a noisy world, visibility wins. But smart visibility – fueled by story, strategy, and service – wins bigger."

Mastering PR means mastering the art of being found by opportunity, not just chasing it.

CHAPTER 10

PERSONAL AND TEAM DEVELOPMENT TOOLS

> *Excellence isn't achieved once. It's engineered daily. Your systems build your future.*

Why You Need Systems for Personal and Team Growth

Success in sales doesn't happen by accident – it happens by design.

Top sellers and teams are relentless about tracking, measuring, and improving their performance across multiple time horizons: Daily, Weekly, Quarterly, and Semi-Annually.

Without personal accountability tools, you drift. With them, you dominate.

Big Idea:

"Consistency beats intensity. Systems beat motivation."

DAILY – Personal Battle Boards

Example 1: Classic Battle Board

Metric	Daily target	Actual
New Prospects Contacted	5	6
Follow-Ups Sent	5	5
Meetings Set	2	1
Meetings Held	1	1
Learning (Minutes)	30 min	30 min

Visual Tip: Use whiteboards, notebooks, or simple Excel sheets. Keep it visible.

Place Your Logo here

BATTLE BOARD
Fall 202X

PLAY LIKE A CHAMPION / FIRST TO GET ANGRY LOSES / DO WHAT OTHERS WON'T / VISUALIZE SUCCESS / WRITE DOWN THE PLAN / COMMUNICATE THE PLAN / TAKE THE NEXT STEP / ACTION OVER IDEAS / QUESTION ANYTHING / IMPROVE EVERYTHING / TALK LESS / DO MORE

TODAY
1
2
3

THIS WEEK
1
2
3
4
5
6
7
8

HR/ STAFFING/ ADMIN
A
A
A
B
B
B
C
C
C

MARKETING/ RESEARCH/ EVENTS
1
2
3
4
5
6

PERSONAL GROWTH (IDEAS/ BOOKS)
1
2
3
4
5
6

TECH/ INFRASTRUCTURE1
A
A
A
B
B
C

SALES MINDSET
1. Be Nice. New Biz Daily. Bring Solutions.
2. 5/5/30
3. 6 Months Out Selling. ABM and Marketing
4. Legacy clients move to Act. Mngt.
5. Annuals, Upfronts, Advisory Board

BUSINESS #1
1
2
3
4
5
6
7
8
9
10
11
12

BUSINESS #2
1
2
3
4
5
6
7
8
9
10
11
12

BUSINESS #3
1
2
3
4
5
6
7
8
9
10
11
12

BUSINESS #4
1
2
3
4
5
6
7
8
9
10
11
12

Priority #1	Priority #4
Priority #2	Priority #5
Priority #3	Priority #6

Example 2: Digital Battle Board (CRM/Apps)

- HubSpot Task Lists

- Monday.com Daily Boards

- Trello "Daily Flow" Columns

Pro Tip:
End each day with a 2-minute review: *"Did I win today?" If not, why?*

WEEKLY – Quick Report
(Even if Only for Personal Use)

What to Include in a Weekly Quick Report:

1. Deals Won
2. Deals Moved Forward
3. New Leads Added
4. Key Lessons Learned
5. Top 3 Priorities for Next Week

Weekly Report Example Format:

Wins:

- Closed $45K new business.
- Booked meeting with Delta.

Pipeline Movement:

Moved 3 deals to contract stage.

New Leads:

7 qualified leads from LinkedIn.

Lessons:

Better early budget qualification needed.

Next Week:

- Focus on 2 expansion accounts.
- Prep for industry webinar.

[**Your Logo here**]   *[NAME OF SELLER] WEEKLY REPORT*

TOP 5 ITEMS ACCOMPLISHED THIS WEEK	TOP 5 ITEMS FOR NEXT WEEK
1)	1)
2)	2)
3)	3)
4)	4)
5)	5)

TOP NEEDS	TOP RISKS
1)	1)
2)	2)
3)	3)

	MONDAY	TUESDAY	WEDNESDAY	THURSDAY	FRIDAY
TOP 5 DAILY PROSPECTS					
TOP 5 DAILY FOLLOW-UPS					

MEETING AND EVENTS	UPCOMING MEETINGS		PIPELINE AND DEAL SNAPSHOT	TOP 5 DEALS WORKING TO CLOSE
	1)			1)
	2)			2)
	3)			3)
	4)			4)
	5)			5)
	UPCOMING EVENTS/ CONFERENCES			TOP 5 MOST RECENT DEALS CLOSED
	1)			1)

Golden Rule:

If you write it down weekly, you won't lose sight of your quarter's endgame.

QUARTERLY – Sales Velocity

Calculator (Use Before New Q)

[**Your Logo here**]

SALES VELOCITY
KEY= Update Five Light Gray Cells Only

| | #of Deals x Average Deal Size x % Win Rate | | | |
	Length of Sales Cycle (Months)			
Current Sales Velocity				
#of Deals in Pipeline	Avg. Deal Size	% Win Rate	Velocity	% Improvement
30	$ 50,000	50%	$ 375,000	
2				
Length of Sales Cycle (Months)				48%
New Sales Velocity				
10%				
33	$ 55,000	55%	$ 554,583	
1.8				

$179,000 IMPROVEMENT

NOTES:

1. *Focus on getting the right prospects, not just any prospects*
2. *Increase avg. deal value/ size*
3. *Increase win rate %*
4. *Reduce time needed to close each deal*

Sales Velocity Formula:

Sales Velocity = (Number of Opportunities × Deal Value × Win Rate) ÷ Sales Cycle Length

Quarterly Prep Example:

Metric	Last Quarter	Target Next Quarter
# of Opportunities	40	50
Average Deal Size	$10,000	$12,000
Win Rate	25%	30%
Sales Cycle (Days)	45	40

Insights You Can Gain:

- Where do you need to increase volume?
- Where can you raise deal size?
- How can you speed up decision cycles?

Pro Tip:

Sales is math. Play the right math game, and you'll predictably crush your goals.

QUARTERLY – Seller Scorecard

Scorecard Categories:

Category	Metrics to Track
Revenue Performance	% of goal achieved
Prospecting Discipline	Daily outreach averages
Meeting Conversion Rate	Meetings -> Opportunities
Follow-Up Speed	Avg. response time
Client Retention	Renewal/expansion rates

FY 20XX SELLER SCORECARD
<NAME OF SALESPERSON>

QUARTER	MEASURE	NOTES	GOAL	ACTUAL	RESULT	WEIGHT	Q1 SCORE
Q1	Sales Revenue (Performance)	Individual Goal	$450,000	$500,000	111%	1.00	11.11
	#Pipeline Deals (Effectiveness)	Maintain 30 Deals / Each Day	30	25	83%	0.60	5.00
	#of New Outbonds (Effectiveness)	5 New Outbonds / Day - 300 / Quarter	300	100	33%	0.20	0.67
	Biz Dev (Effectiveness)	5 Follow - Ups / Day - 300 / Quarter	300	100	33%	0.20	0.67
	Performance (10 = Score Goal)						**10.00**
	Effectiveness (10 = Score Goal)						**6.3**
Q2	Sales Revenue (Performance)	Individual Goal	$450,000	$500,000	111%	1.00	11.11
	#Pipeline Deals (Effectiveness)	Maintain 30 Deals / Each Day	30	25	83%	0.60	5.00
	#of New Outbonds (Effectiveness)	5 New Outbonds / Day - 300 / Quarter	300	100	33%	0.20	0.67
	Biz Dev (Effectiveness)	5 Follow - Ups / Day - 300 / Quarter	300	100	33%	0.20	0.67
	Performance (10 = Score Goal)						**10.00**
	Effectiveness (10 = Score Goal)						**6.3**
Q3	Sales Revenue (Performance)	Individual Goal	$450,000	$500,000	111%	1.00	11.11
	#Pipeline Deals (Effectiveness)	Maintain 30 Deals / Each Day	30	25	83%	0.60	5.00
	#of New Outbonds (Effectiveness)	5 New Outbonds / Day - 300 / Quarter	300	100	33%	0.20	0.67
	Biz Dev (Effectiveness)	5 Follow - Ups / Day - 300 / Quarter	300	100	33%	0.20	0.67
	Performance (10 = Score Goal)						**10.00**
	Effectiveness (10 = Score Goal)						**6.3**
Q4	Sales Revenue (Performance)	Individual Goal	$450,000	$500,000	111%	1.00	11.11
	#Pipeline Deals (Effectiveness)	Maintain 30 Deals / Each Day	30	25	83%	0.60	5.00
	#of New Outbonds (Effectiveness)	5 New Outbonds / Day - 300 / Quarter	300	100	33%	0.20	0.67
	Biz Dev (Effectiveness)	5 Follow - Ups / Day - 300 / Quarter	300	100	33%	0.20	0.67
	Performance (10 = Score Goal)						**10.00**
	Effectiveness (10 = Score Goal)						**6.3**

Build a personal Seller Scorecard every quarter – treat yourself like a pro athlete.

Self-Grading Tip:

A simple A–B–C score works:

- **A** = Exceptional
- **B** = Solid but room for growth
- **C** = Needs immediate improvement

Example Self-Scorecard Entry:

Category	Score	Note
Prospecting	B	Hitting 80% of targets
Follow-Up	A	Same-day responses 90% of time
Client Retention	C	Lost 2 key accounts, need better onboarding follow-up

QUARTERLY – If You Have Budget for Paid Media – Use It!

Paid Media for Personal Brand or Company Awareness:

- LinkedIn Sponsored Posts
- Google Ads (targeting specific verticals)
- Facebook/Instagram (for B2C)
- Industry Newsletters (like Defense News, TechCrunch)

Where to Start with Paid Media:

- Start small: $250–$500/month.
- Promote gated content (e.g., whitepapers, webinars).
- Retarget website visitors with low-cost ads.

Pro Tip:

Paid media isn't just for brand awareness — it can build your personal pipeline too.

[**Your Logo here**]

MARKETING BUDGET FOR DGTL AND OFFLINE
FALL 202X

DIGITAL MKTG.	Jan	Feb	Mar	Apr	May	Jun	Jul	Aug	Sep	Oct	Nov	Dec	YEARLY TOTAL
Website													
Blogs													
SEO / SEM													
Email newsletters													
Google AdWords													
Geographical advertising (e.g. Google Places)													
Affiliate marketing													
Facebook													
Twitter													
YouTube													
LinkedIn													
Instagram													
TikTok													
Online press releases													
Online reputation management													
Mobile Apps (iPhone / Android)													
Text / SMS													
Bluetooth location-based marketing													
Augmented reality													
ONLINE SUB-TOTAL													

OFFLINE MKTG.	Jan	Feb	Mar	Apr	May	Jun	Jul	Aug	Sep	Oct	Nov	Dec	YEARLY TOTAL
Direct mail													
Print advertising													
Broadcast advertising													
OOH - Events - Locations													
Merchandising & point of sale													
Telemarketing													
Networking													
Case studies / Testimonials													
Awards													
Trade shows & exhibitions													
Corporate events													
Endorsements													
Sponsorship													
Interviews / Media presence													
Speeches & presentations													
Articles for publication													
Press releases / News													
Public relations & publicity													
The personal touch (e.g. cards & gifts)													
OFFLINE SUB-TOTAL													
TOTAL (ONLINE & OFFLINE)													

[YOUR LOGO HERE]

To create more than one line of text within a cell, simply hold down 'Alt' while you press 'Return' if you're using a PC or to a Mac press 'Ctrl' 'Alt' and 'Return'

	January	February	March	April	May	June	July	August	September	October	November	December
Your Key Campaigns or Events	Add your key calendar or campaign milestones											
Any Special Offers & Sales Promotions	Add your offers and promotions											
DIGITAL MKTG.	January	February	March	April	May	June	July	August	September	October	November	December
Website	Short desc. of planned mktg											
Blogs												
SEO / SEM												
Email newsletters												
Google AdWords												
Geographical advertising (e.g. Google Places)												
Affiliate marketing												
Online business directories & listings												
Facebook												
Twitter												
YouTube												
LinkedIn												
Instagram												
TikTok												
Online press releases												
Online reputation management												
Mobile Apps (iPhone / Android)												
Text / SMS												
Bluetooth location-based marketing												
Augmented reality												

247

[YOUR LOGO HERE]

OFFLINE MARKETING PLAN
FALL 202X

To create more than one line of text within a cell, simply hold down 'Alt' while you press 'Return' if you're using a PC or for a Mac press 'Ctrl', 'Alt' and 'Return'

	January	February	March	April	May	June	July	August	September	October	November	December
Your Key Campaigns of Events	Add your key calendar or campaign milestones											
Any Special Offers & Sales Promotions	Add your offers and promotions											
OFFLINE MKTG.	Short desc. of planned mktg.											
Direct mail												
Print advertising												
Broadcast advertising												
OOH - Events - Locations												
Merchandising & point of sale												
Personal selling												
Telemarketing												
Networking												
Referrals												
Case studies / Testimonials												
Awards												
Trade shows & exhibitions												
Corporate events												
Other events												
Endorsements												
Sponsorship												
Interviews / Media presence												
Speeches & presentations												
Articles for publication												
Press releases / News												
Public relations & publicity												
The personal touch (e.g. cards & gifts)												

Semi-Annually – Self Review

Name: <Name>   Date of Review: x/x/20xx

Are the expectations for your position clear?
Any items to call out?

<Enter Your Info Here>

What areas do you feel you need to improve
upon to beat your 20xx goals?

<Enter Your Info Here>

What accomplishment(s) are you
most proud of during 20xx?

<Enter Your Info Here>

What training or assistance would you like

<Enter Your Info Here>

Self-Review Core Questions:

1. What was my proudest achievement?

2. Where did I fall short – and why?

3. Which skill improved most? Which needs the most work?

4. Am I happier, more skilled, and more connected than six
   months ago?

5. What is my next big goal?

Bonus:

Create a "highlight reel" of wins from the past 6 months – even private notes boost morale.

Semi-Annually – Manager Review

If You Manage Others:

Manager Review Core Topics:

- Revenue vs. Goal
- Key Wins + Key Challenges
- Skill Development Progress
- Next Quarter Focus Areas
- Personal/Professional Growth Feedback

Simple Manager 1-Pager Review Format:

Area	Feedback
Strengths	[List 2–3 strengths]
Growth Areas	[List 2–3 areas for improvement]
Action Plan	[What support is needed next?]

Pro Tip:

Feedback should be specific, supportive, and tied to behaviors, not personalities.

Name:	<Name>		% To Individual Sales Goal	Q1	88%
Title:	<Title>			Q2	90%
Today's Date:	12/15/2022			Q3	95%
Date of Hire:	2/1/2018			Q4	107%
Years in Position:	4.87			20xx	95%
Date of Review	8/22/2022				

DRIVE & FOCUS

Self Motivated	4
Positive Attitude	4
Go Above and Beyond Role	3
Attention to Detail	3
SECTION RATING	**3.5**

SALES PROCESS

Comfort Describing All of our Products	3
Can Easily Develop Sponsorship Ideas	3
Hits or Beats Quarterly Revenue Goals	1
30+ Deals Always in Pipeline	3
Earn Premium Rates and CPMs	4
CRM Knowledge & Ability	3
Utilize CRM for All Deal / Campaign Activiy	3
SECTION RATING	**2.9**

LEADERSHIP SKILLS

Stays Calm in Conflict	4
Comfortable Asking for Help	4
Comfortable Delegating	4
Comfortable Managing Up	4
Develops Plans to Hit or Beat Sales Goals	2
Team Player / Positive Influence	3
SECTION RATING	**3.5**

EXTERNAL COMMUNICATION

Comfortable Telling Company Story	3
Comfortable Cold Calling	3
Regularly Builds Custom Decks for Pitches	3
Emails Short and Easily Understandable	3
Completes 5 New Business Outbounds / Day	3
SECTION RATING	**3.0**

INTERNAL COMMUNICATION

Readily Works with Support Teams	3
Communicates with other Reps on Deals	3
Follows Process to get Deals Done	3
SECTION RATING	**3.0**

RANKING DEFINITIONS

5 = Consistently Exceeds Expectations

4 = Exceeds Expectations

3 = Achieves Expectations

2 = Meets Some Expectations

1 = Does Not Meet Expectations

OVERALL RATING	**3.2**

Manager Comments:

Workshop Activities

1. Battle Board Design Sprint

- Design your Daily Battle Board on paper or digitally.
- Track it for 14 straight days.
- Measure daily wins and blockers.

2. Sales Velocity Calculation Challenge

- Use last quarter's real numbers.
- Calculate your sales velocity.
- Set realistic improvement targets for each variable next quarter.

3. Self-Review Journal Entry

Write a semi-annual self-review answering:

- What did I do better than expected?
- Where did I surprise myself?
- What is the one big upgrade I must make next?

Bonus Tips

- Visual trackers beat hidden trackers. Make it visible = make it happen.
- Gamify personal goals — 5% improvement each quarter compounds into >20% growth annually.
- Have a "Personal Board of Advisors" — mentors, friends, trusted colleagues who can give honest feedback.
- Review weekly + monthly patterns, not just quarterly summaries — tiny corrections now = major wins later.

Final Thought

"Systems create freedom. Discipline creates dominance."

Master your own development tools — and you won't just survive the sales game. You'll build a career that scales with you, not against you.

CHAPTER 11

IF THERE IS A REVENUE GAP, FIND IT. FIX IT.

"

Revenue gaps aren't failures — they're flashing arrows pointing toward your next level of growth. Follow them.

"

Why Closing Revenue Gaps is a Critical Skill

Revenue gaps don't appear overnight – they build slowly, through small problems left unchecked.

The best sellers and sales teams hunt for gaps before they become chasms. They fix issues fast. They treat pipeline health like elite athletes treat injuries: Immediate diagnosis. Immediate action.

Big Idea:

"Revenue gaps are not bad luck. They are solvable problems – if you're brave enough to find and fix them early."

Where is the Problem?

What Are Your Best Practices?

Diagnosing Revenue Gaps Quickly:

SYMPTOM	POSSIBLE ROOT CAUSE	EXAMPLE
Not enough meetings	Weak top-of-funnel prospecting	50% fewer outreach activities than prior quarter
Meetings, but no proposals	Poor qualification or unclear discovery process	Not asking budget/timeline questions early
PROPOSALS, BUT NO WINS	Poor value articulation or weak competitive differentiation	Proposal is feature-focused, not outcome-focused
Wins, but no upsells/renewals	Poor onboarding or lack of customer nurturing	No follow-up strategy after initial sale

Best Practice:

Don't guess where the gap is. Measure it across the full sales funnel.

Funnel Stage	Metrics to Review
Prospecting	Number of outreach activities per week
First Meetings	Conversion rate from outreach to meeting
Opportunities Created	% of meetings leading to qualified opportunities
Win Rate	% of proposals turning into wins
Revenue Per Deal	Average contract size vs. goal
Customer Retention	Renewal rates, upsell rates

Don't Wait for Clients to Show You the Problem

The Danger of Passive Selling:

- Hoping the client "tells you" something is wrong

- Waiting for budgets to shrink or priorities to shift without proactive conversations

Be Proactive:

Action	Why It Matters
Regular QBRs (Quarterly Business Reviews)	Stay top-of-mind and uncover hidden dissatisfaction early
Customer Health Checks	Identify churn risk before it's too late
Post-Sale Surveys	Immediate insight on onboarding experience and NPS (Net Promoter Score)
Deal Retrospectives (Lost Deal Reviews)	Spot recurring themes you can fix

Example Questions to Uncover Early Problems:

- *"If you could wave a magic wand, what would you change about our solution?"*

- *"What's one thing we could do better to support your success this quarter?"*

- *"What has surprised you most – good or bad – since working with us?"*

Pro Tip:

Customers rarely offer negative feedback unprompted. Exceptional sellers invite feedback early, so fixes are easy – not emergency rescues later.

Recap of Key Items to Drive Revenue

Find the Gap Fast:

- Watch funnel conversion rates weekly.
- Notice small shifts before they become big swings.

Own the Problem (Even if You Didn't Cause It):

- No finger-pointing. No excuses.
- Always ask: What can I control? What can I fix immediately?

Double-Down on Proven Best Practices:

- Prospect daily – never stop filling your pipeline.
- Prep hard for every customer meeting.
- Always confirm next steps (in writing) after every conversation.
- Track your metrics weekly, not quarterly.
- Follow up faster than your competition.
- Invest extra time in customer onboarding and relationship nurturing.

Golden Rule:
"Don't lose deals for preventable reasons."

Workshop Activities

1. Revenue Gap Finder Drill

- Sketch your full funnel from top to bottom.
- Write real numbers for:
  - » Prospects contacted
  - » Meetings booked
  - » Opportunities created
  - » Proposals sent
  - » Deals won
- Identify the biggest drop-off stage.
- Brainstorm 3 immediate actions to fix it.

2. Client Feedback Sprint

- Pick 5 current customers.
- Send a 2-question check-in email:
  - » *"What's working really well for you right now?"*
  - » *"What could we improve to make your experience even better?"*
- Analyze responses and take immediate corrective action.

3. Sales Funnel Improvement Sprint

- Choose one funnel stage you want to improve next quarter.
- Set a micro-goal tied to that stage.

Example Micro-Goal:

"If I book 10% more qualified first meetings per month, my pipeline will increase by $50K."

- **Build a daily/weekly plan to hit it.**

Bonus Tips

- **Pipeline problems are pipeline problems** – not proposal problems.

- **Always assume churn risk is higher than it looks.**

- **Look at win/loss reasons monthly. Document common objections** – solve the root causes, not just symptoms.

- **Celebrate small improvements**. Fixing a 5% leakage at one stage can drive 15–20% more revenue over a year.

Final Thought

"Amateurs blame outcomes. Professionals fix systems."

The faster you find your revenue gaps – and the faster you act to close them – the bigger your advantage will be over sellers who just hope the quarter turns around.

Hope isn't a strategy. **Fixing the gaps is.**

CHAPTER 12

ADDITIONAL RESOURCES TO IMPROVE YOUR REVENUE

> *The ultimate sales system starts with the ultimate sales machine – you.*
> *Invest accordingly.*

Why You Are Your Greatest Revenue-Generating Asset

Revenue doesn't just come from hard work.

It comes from your **energy**, your **mindset**, your **daily discipline**, and your ability to **show up fully, consistently, and relentlessly.**

If you want a bigger paycheck, you must first build a **stronger you.**

> **Big Idea:**
> "Your mind and body are your real sales tools — treat them like million-dollar assets."

Your Health! No One Else Is Going To Do This For You

Sales is a Full-Contact Sport. It demands energy, resilience, and clarity.

If your health declines:

- Your energy sags.
- Your focus fades.
- Your emotional resilience crumbles.
- Your customers feel it — even if you think you're hiding it.

Health Foundations for Sales Success:

Habit	Why It Matters
Sleep 7–8 hours	Boosts mental sharpness, creativity, and patience
Exercise 4–5x a week	Builds endurance and mood stability
Hydration & Nutrition	Fuels brain function and physical stamina
Stress Management	Reduces burnout risk and emotional reactivity

Pro Tip:

You are a corporate athlete. Prepare and recover like one.

Be Relentless!

Relentlessness isn't about working 24/7. It's about refusing to quit when things get difficult or tedious.

What Relentless Sellers Do:

- Prospect every day – even when pipeline looks "good enough."
- Follow up more times than feels comfortable.
- Prepare for meetings like every one could be career-defining.
- Seek feedback constantly.
- Never let small losses erode their big-picture confidence.

Example:

The average seller follows up 1–2 times. Top performers follow up **5–8 times** – without being annoying – by always adding value.

How to Train Relentlessness:

- Set micro-goals: "Send 5 prospecting emails even after a bad day."

- Use visual trackers: Watch your streaks grow.

- Reward effort, not just outcomes: Celebrate the days you outworked your fear.

Reminder: Do 5 Outbounds and 5 Follow-Ups Every Day

5 + 5 Discipline:

Task	Why It Matters
5 Outbound Contacts	Keeps pipeline growing
5 Follow-Up Messages	Advances deals already in progress

Visual Tracker Example:

Day	5 New	5 Follow-up	Total Conversations
Monday	√	√	7
Tuesday	√	√	5

Pro Tip:

Miss one day? Double up the next day. Discipline compounds faster than motivation.

Golden Rule:

The day you stop outbounding and following up is the day your future revenue starts dying.

Workshop Activities

1. Health Investment Plan

Write 3 daily health habits you will commit to for the next 30 days. Example:

- 7 hours minimum sleep.
- Walk 20 minutes daily.
- 2 liters of water daily.

Goal:
Treat your body like a revenue-producing machine.

2. Relentlessness Challenge

- Choose one day this week where you feel tired, overwhelmed, or unmotivated.
- That day, commit to completing your 5+5 anyway — no excuses.

Reflection Prompt Afterward:
How did you feel when you finished anyway?

3. 5+5 Daily Tracker

- Set up a simple grid in your journal, Google Sheet, or whiteboard.

- Every day for 30 days:

  » Mark "√" after 5 new outreaches.

  » Mark "√" after 5 follow-ups.

  » Watch your momentum grow visually.

Optional Bonus:

Share your streak with a peer or mentor for extra accountability.

Bonus Tips

- Energy is a sales multiplier. A 5% energy boost often leads to 15–20% better meetings.

- Follow-up until you hear "no" — not until you hear nothing.

- Remember: Burnout comes from misalignment, not hard work. Focus on meaningful daily wins.

- Adopt the "Two-Minute Rule": If a small action takes less than 2 minutes (like a quick follow-up email), do it immediately.

Final Thought

"Revenue growth starts in your mind, builds through your habits, and compounds through your resilience."

If you relentlessly protect your health, your effort, and your discipline, there is no market condition, no economic downturn, no competitor that can stop you.

You become unstoppable because you've mastered the only thing that truly matters: **yourself.**

STRAIGHT UP SELLING — THE JOURNEY TO EXCEPTIONALISM

“

Congratulations — You've made it through Straight Up Selling — not just another sales book, but a real blueprint for **building an unstoppable revenue career.**

”

You've learned that selling isn't about slick words or lucky breaks. It's about systems, discipline, preparation, resilience, and most of all — ownership.

You now have a full toolkit:

- A sales process that starts with prospecting and scales into partnerships.
- A mindset that transforms setbacks into springboards.
- A battle-tested daily discipline that drives predictable success.
- A customer-first communication style that builds trust and loyalty.
- Personal development systems that guarantee long-term career acceleration.

The Straight Up Selling Mantras to Remember:

- Revenue is the outcome. Sales is the process.
- Own the pipeline. Own the meeting. Own the follow-up.
- Prepare better than your competition.
- Control your attitude, effort, and self-development — every single day.
- Relentlessness beats raw talent when talent slacks off.
- No one will care about your goals as much as you do — and that's exactly how it should be.

The Future Is Wide Open

This is not the end of your journey — it's the beginning of a new level of performance. Because now you know:

Exceptional sellers aren't born. They are built.

You are building yourself with every email you send, every meeting you prep for, every follow-up call you make, every ounce of discipline you invest when no one else is watching.

Straight Up Selling isn't about hoping for success.

It's about **engineering success** – step-by-step, habit-by-habit, win-by-win.

Final Charge

- **Stay coachable.** Every deal – win or lose – has a lesson inside.

- **Stay consistent.** Your future is being built in your daily rituals.

- **Stay courageous.** The best opportunities are just past the first "no."

- **Stay humble.** Confidence and humility are not opposites – they are partners.

- **Stay relentless.** Ordinary effort guarantees ordinary results. You're here for more.

And remember: The number you're chasing today is not just a quota. It's your next opportunity to prove to yourself what you are capable of. **Straight Up Selling is not something you do for one quarter. It's how you lead, compete, and win for an entire career**. Now get out there. **Go make something exceptional happen.**

APPENDIX
STRAIGHT UP SELLING:
RECOMMENDED READING LIST

SECTION 1: INTRODUCTION — Revenue vs. Sales

- *Atomic Habits* by **James Clear** — Build systems, not goals.

- *The Sales Acceleration Formula* by **Mark Roberge** — Data-driven sales process building.

- *The Ultimate Sales Machine* by **Chet Holmes** — Focusing on repeatable excellence.

SECTION 2: Scaling Outreach to Beat Your Revenue Goals

- *Fanatical Prospecting* by **Jeb Blount** — Mastering daily outreach discipline.

- *Predictable Revenue* by **Aaron Ross** — Systematizing outbound sales.

- *Sell It Like Serhant* by **Ryan Serhant** — High-energy prospecting and follow-up.

SECTION 3: How to Find the Best Prospects and Stand Out

- *New Sales. Simplified.* by **Mike Weinberg** — Targeting and messaging fundamentals.

- *SPIN Selling* by **Neil Rackham** — Advanced questioning to uncover needs.

- *Influence: The Psychology of Persuasion* by **Robert Cialdini** — Standing out through behavioral science.

SECTION 4: Sales Writing & Employing Empathy

- *Everybody Writes* by **Ann Handley** – Clear, effective business writing.

- *Exactly What to Say* by **Phil M. Jones** – Magic words for sales conversations.

- *Words That Sell* by **Richard Bayan** – Crafting powerful, action-driven copy.

SECTION 5: Put in the Time Before, During & After Meetings

- *Never Split the Difference* by **Chris Voss** – Negotiation mastery through tactical empathy.

- *The Coaching Habit* by **Michael Bungay Stanier** – Ask better questions in meetings.

- *Take the Cold Out of Cold Calling* by **Sam Richter** – Pre-call research that changes outcomes.

SECTION 6: "The Nine Tool" To Inform Your Sales Process

- *The Challenger Sale* by **Matthew Dixon and Brent Adamson** – Teaching and tailoring in complex deals.

- *To Sell Is Human* by **Daniel Pink** – Modern psychology of influencing.

- *Insight Selling* by **Mike Schultz and John Doerr** – Leading with customer-centric insights.

SECTION 7: Forging Exceptionalism

- *Relentless* by **Tim Grover** – Mindset of champions.

- *Grit* by **Angela Duckworth** – The power of passion

and perseverance.

- *Mindset* by **Carol Dweck** – Developing a growth mindset for long-term excellence.

SECTION 8: Maximizing Communication – LLTQC

- *Crucial Conversations* by **Kerry Patterson et al.** – Handling high-stakes conversations.

- *The Art of Active Listening* by **Heather Younger** – Mastering the core skill of listening.

- *Exactly How to Sell* by **Phil M. Jones** – Communication sequences for success.

SECTION 9: Seven-Step PR to Gain Inbound Leads and Drive Revenue

- *Building a StoryBrand* by **Donald Miller** – Clarifying your company's message.

- *Trust Me, I'm Lying* by **Ryan Holiday** – Understanding the media game.

- *Content Inc.* by **Joe Pulizzi** – Content marketing for inbound growth.

SECTION 10: Personal & Team Development Tools

- *The 5AM Club* by **Robin Sharma** – Winning your day early.

- *The One Thing* by **Gary Keller and Jay Papasan** – Focus and discipline in work and life.

- *Extreme Ownership* by **Jocko Willink and Leif Babin** – Leadership and personal responsibility at every level.

SECTION 11: If There Is a Revenue Gap, Find It. Fix It.

- *Measure What Matters* by **John Doerr** – Using OKRs to find and close performance gaps.

- *The Sales Development Playbook* by **Trish Bertuzzi** – Pipeline creation as a science.

- *Eat Their Lunch* by **Anthony Iannarino** – Winning customers in competitive markets.

SECTION 12: Additional Resources to Improve YOUR Revenue

- *Can't Hurt Me* by **David Goggins** – Mastering mental toughness.

- *High Performance Habits* by **Brendon Burchard** – Personal systems for sustainable success.

- *The Slight Edge* by **Jeff Olson** – The power of daily improvements compounded over time.

BOOK 4

PEOPLE DRIVE REVENUE

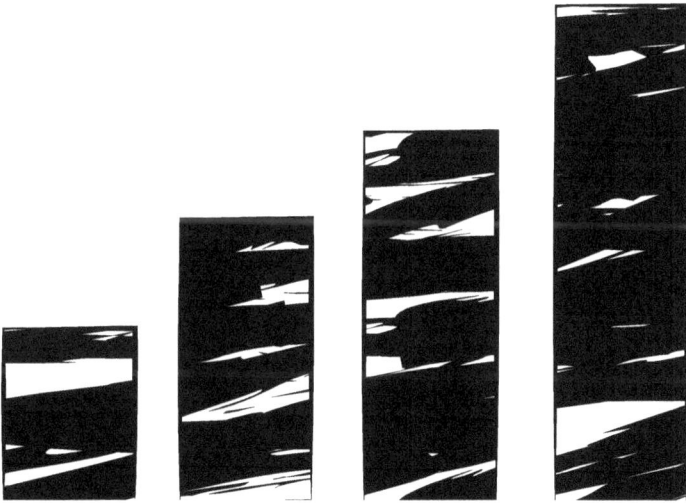

TALENT SYSTEMS THAT DELIVER RESULTS

TABLE OF CONTENTS

INTRODUCTION

People Drive Revenue

Revenue doesn't come from spreadsheets, pipelines, or comp plans. It comes from people. Every single time.

Behind every closed deal, every quarterly surge, every market expansion – is a seller who delivered. A manager who coached. A leader who hired right. And yet, far too many sales organizations focus all their energy on products, pricing, and promotions, while treating talent as an afterthought.

This book is a correction. A reset. A roadmap.

People Drive Revenue is not just about hiring more reps or training harder. It's about building a **system** that attracts top performers, grows them, holds them accountable, and retains them – while protecting your team from the costly drift of mediocrity.

Inside, you'll find ten no-fluff chapters packed with real-world strategies for:

1. Avoiding bad hires before they hit your payroll

2. Creating scalable hiring and performance frameworks

3. Promoting the right people into leadership (and avoiding the wrong ones)

4. Letting go of low performers with speed, fairness, and clarity

5. Building a permanent recruiting bench so you're never caught scrambling

Whether you lead a team of five or 500, this book will give you the tools to make your s**ales talent your competitive**

advantage. Because the truth is simple:

You don't have a revenue problem. You have a people system problem.

Let's fix that – and unlock the revenue waiting on the other side.

CHAPTER 1

THE SALES TALENT FORMULA

> *You can't build a revenue engine on the wrong people, no matter how good your process is. Great sellers make systems work — not the other way around.*

Introduction: Your System Is Only as Strong as Your People

Sales leaders love process. We build sales funnels, forecast pipelines, track KPIs, and analyze close rates. And yet, the majority of revenue issues stem not from bad processes – but from **bad people decisions.**

It's easy to believe that with the right script, training deck, or CRM setup, you can turn any warm body into a seller. But in reality, **revenue is a reflection of the people executing the system** – not just the system itself.

So before you optimize workflows or adopt the latest enablement tool, ask a more important question:

Do I have the right people on the field?

This chapter will show you how to assess, hire, retain, and, when necessary, remove the people who determine whether your revenue strategy wins or fails.

The Real Cost of Hiring the Wrong Seller

Let's break it down:

Bad hire math

- Salary & benefits: $85,000
- Onboarding & training: $7,500
- Missed revenue over 6–9 months: $300,000+

- Team disruption & morale damage: incalculable

One bad hire = 6–12 months of lost growth.

Hiring without a system is the equivalent of giving someone a sales quota with no product, no pitch, and no plan. Yet this happens in companies all the time.

What Makes a Great Seller?

Traits to Hire For – Not Just Hope For

"Top sellers don't just hit quota – they build relationships, solve problems, and elevate everyone around them."

5 Core Traits of High-Performing Sales Talent:

1. **Coachability** – They absorb feedback and improve fast.

   ■ **Tip:** Ask: "Tell me about a time you changed your approach after feedback."

2. **Accountability** – They own their number like they own the business.

   ■ **Tip:** Ask: "When you missed quota, what did you change immediately?"

3. **Process Discipline** – They follow the system, not their ego.

   ■ **Example:** Top sellers log activity, follow stages, and use CRM properly – without being micromanaged.

4. **Intellectual Curiosity** – They want to understand the customer, not just pitch the product.

Tip: Listen for smart, specific questions during the interview.

5. **Integrity** – They close clean and keep promises.

Example: If someone glosses over losses or blames others, dig deeper.

Red Flags to Watch For

in Interviews

- Talks only about big wins, never about failure
- Blames *"bad leads,"* *"bad managers,"* or *"bad territories"*
- Over-focuses on comp plans, under-focuses on value creation
- Doesn't ask insightful questions about your business

One interview tip:
Replace *"Tell me"* with *"Walk me through."*
This forces real stories, not rehearsed clichés.

The Jack Welch Talent Matrix for Sales

Adapted from GE's leadership model, here's how to evaluate your team:

PERFORMANCE	CULTURE FIT	CATEGORY	ACTION
High	High	Top Performer	Promote, protect, reward
High	Low	Toxic Closer	Exit before damage spreads
Low	High	Coachable	Invest and give a plan
Low	Low	Misfit	Remove quickly

You must protect the team from toxicity as much as you protect revenue.

Real-World Example: When the Right Hire Changed Everything

A cybersecurity SaaS company hired a quiet, analytical former engineer as an AE. On paper, he lacked "classic sales swagger." But in the first quarter, he outperformed the top three reps by focusing obsessively on solving client problems, not pitching features.

Result:

He closed more deals — with bigger contract values — and is now the regional VP.

Why?

Because **he was the right who** – and he made the how better just by showing up.

Workshop Activities

Activity 1: Build Your Sales Talent Scorecard

Instructions:

Create your own scorecard using the following criteria. Rank each from 1–5.

TRAIT	WEIGHT	SCORE (1-5)	NOTES
Coachability	High		
Process Discipline	High		
Curiosity	Medium		
Culture Alignment	High		
Communication	Medium		

Discuss with your team:

- What traits matter most in your company's culture and product cycle?

- Are you screening for these or just selling the role?

Activity 2: Audit Your Current Team Using the Welch Matrix

- Step 1: Put every rep in one of the four quadrants.

- Step 2: Define a plan of action for each quadrant.

- Step 3: Meet with your managers and set timelines – don't let analysis lead to inaction.

- **Rule of thumb:** If you wouldn't enthusiastically rehire them today, it's time for a change.

Chapter Conclusion:
Right People > Right Process

Here's the hard truth:

Even your best-designed sales system will fail if the wrong people are running it.

The reps you hire – and the managers you promote – determine not just the numbers, but the morale, retention, and future of your business.

The best leaders don't just build processes. **They build teams.** And the best sales teams don't just hit quota. **They build revenue engines.**

You can buy tools. You can adopt frameworks. But there is no substitute for great people who show up every day to win, improve, and lead.

Start with who. The rest will follow.

CHAPTER 2

JACK WELCH REVISITED

> *Protect your stars. Coach the willing. Remove the toxic. That's how you build a team that wins on purpose.*

Introduction: Why Every Team Fails Without a People Strategy

You don't need to be a Fortune 500 CEO to apply world-class leadership frameworks. In fact, one of the most powerful management models ever created came from **Jack Welch**, former CEO of GE, who led the company to massive growth by focusing relentlessly on **people clarity**.

Welch simplified the complexity of talent management into four quadrants. His advice was clear:

- **Promote the best.**

- **Coach the coachable.**

- **Remove the wrong fit.**

- **Never tolerate toxic winners.**

In sales – where performance is visible and pressure is constant – this model becomes even more powerful. Your success isn't just about who's selling the most today. It's about **who belongs in your locker room long term**.

In this chapter, we'll walk through how to apply Welch's Four Types of Employees specifically to **sales teams** – so you can hire better, coach smarter, and lead with clarity and courage.

The Sales Talent Matrix

The Welch-inspired Sales Talent Matrix plots reps on two key dimensions:

Performance	Cultural Fits/Values
High	The Ideal
High	The Toxic Closer
Low	The Coachable
Low	The Misfit

Let's Break Down Each Type

1. The Ideal: High Performance, High Values

These are your franchise players. They hit quota, help teammates, elevate standards, and represent your brand with integrity.

How to Lead Them:

- Promote them when they're ready – not just when they ask.
- Involve them in mentoring and interviewing.
- Reward their consistency, not just their flash.

Example:

Michelle, a senior AE, consistently exceeds targets. She helps onboard new reps, flags broken systems, and never overpromises to close deals. She builds trust with leadership and clients. She's not just delivering revenue – she's building a revenue culture.

2. The Toxic Closer: High Performance, Low Values

This is the most dangerous person on your team. They often exceed quota but do it in a way that erodes culture, breaks rules, or demoralizes peers.

Symptoms:

- Disrespect toward internal partners (marketing, ops, CS)
- Deals that churn within 90 days
- Drama, cliques, or manipulative behavior

How to Handle:

- Address values violations fast and directly
- Create clear behavior expectations and document them
- If behavior persists, remove them — no matter the revenue

■ "The cost of one toxic closer can outweigh the output of three good reps."

3. The Coachable: Low Performance, High Values

They're trying. They show up early. They ask good questions. But the results just aren't there — yet.

Signs of Coachability:

- Open to feedback and applies it quickly
- Self-aware and emotionally resilient
- Gets better over time, even if slowly

What to Do:

- Put them on a 30–60–90 plan with weekly goals
- Pair them with a top rep
- Set a clear performance bar and timeline

Example:

James was 40% to quota in his first quarter. But his call reviews kept getting better, he asked for extra training, and he improved steadily. By month four, he hit 95%. By month six, he was mentoring others.

4. The Misfit: Low Performance, Low Values

They don't hit numbers. They resist coaching. They blame others. They gossip, disrupt meetings, or quietly lower the bar for everyone.

"You don't have a coaching problem. You have a decision problem."

How to Handle:

- Don't delay. Document behavior and performance.
- Set short-term, measurable improvement targets.
- If no change, exit – quickly and professionally.

Why Managers Avoid These Conversations (And Why That's a Mistake)

Here's why most sales leaders **don't act** when they should:

- *"They might still turn it around."*
- *"They're not that bad."*
- *"It's uncomfortable."*

But here's what happens when you don't act:

- **Your top performers lose respect for you.**

- **Culture turns into chaos.**

- **A-players leave because you tolerate C-level behavior.**

Every minute you keep the wrong person, you disrespect the right ones.

Workshop Activities

Activity 1: Map Your Team in the Matrix

Instructions:

Draw a 2x2 grid with Performance (Low to High) on one axis and Values (Low to High) on the other.

1. Plot each member of your sales team.
2. Discuss as a leadership group:
   » Who are your stars?
   » Who's coachable and worth the effort?
   » Who needs to go?
   » Who's toxic, even if they sell?

Use initials or roles to maintain privacy in team discussions.

Activity 2: Build an Action Plan for Each Quadrant

For each person on your matrix, answer:

- What's the plan?
- What's the timeline?

- Who owns next steps?

■ **Bonus:** Use a shared Google Sheet with manager notes to track progress and accountability.

Chapter Conclusion:
Clarity is Kindness

Jack Welch's framework is still relevant today – especially in sales. It cuts through politics, excuses, and personality traps. It gives you a simple question to ask every month:

"If I had to rehire this person tomorrow, would I?"

If the answer is no – do something. Coach them. Move them. Or remove them.

Remember: You don't just build a revenue machine with top sellers. **You build it with top culture carriers.**

Clarity creates culture. Culture drives behavior. Behavior creates revenue.

Use the matrix. Make the call. Lead your team on purpose.

CHAPTER 3

THE ANATOMY OF A GREAT SELLER

"

Great sellers don't chase deals – they build trust, solve problems, and own outcomes. Sales isn't a personality game. It's a performance craft.

"

Introduction: Top Performers Are Built, Not Born

There's a myth in sales that great sellers are born with charisma, charm, or some unteachable "it factor."

That myth needs to die.

Because in high-performing sales organizations, the most consistent revenue comes not from slick talkers or natural extroverts – it comes from **disciplined, curious, coachable professionals** who operate with purpose.

This chapter breaks down the anatomy of a great seller: the mindset, habits, and behaviors that consistently drive revenue regardless of territory, market, or economy. If you want to hire, develop, or become a top 5% performer, start here.

Core Principle:

Great Sellers Build Systems for Winning

Top sellers don't wing it. They execute a system.

That system may vary in style, tone, or pace – but underneath it are repeatable habits rooted in four key areas.

4 Components of a Great Seller

1. Mindset: The Foundation

"The best sellers see their number like a CEO sees a P&L – it's personal."

Great sellers don't wait to be told what to do. They own their day, own their pipeline, and own the result. They view problems as puzzles, not roadblocks.

Traits:

- Growth mindset
- Resilience under pressure
- Confidence without ego

■ **Example:**

Dee, a medical sales rep, kept losing deals to a competitor. Instead of blaming pricing, she interviewed former prospects to understand why. She rewrote her pitch — and within 90 days, she flipped three major accounts.

2. Process: The Discipline

"Amateurs hope. Pros measure."

Great sellers are process-obsessed. They track deals, follow up religiously, and know exactly what stage each opportunity is in. Their pipeline isn't chaos — it's choreography.

Habits:

- Daily pipeline review
- Weekly activity targets
- Next steps on every deal
- No "ghost" prospects

■ **Tip:** Top sellers never say, *"I think that deal will close."* They say, *"We're in stage four. Legal is reviewing the terms. Close is projected for the 28th."*

3. Customer Obsession: The Differentiator

"Good sellers pitch. Great sellers diagnose."

The best reps know more about the customer's problems than the customer does. They ask sharp, layered questions. They listen more than they speak. They offer insights that change how the buyer thinks.

Example:

Omar, an enterprise SaaS AE, regularly sends prospects articles relevant to their business problems – even if they're not about his product. He's seen as a partner, not a vendor. When budgets tighten, he still gets invited to the table.

Tip:

Use the 3x3 Rule: Before every call, know 3 things about the company and 3 things about the person. Personalization earns attention. Insight earns trust.

4. Execution: The Difference Maker

"In sales, there's no participation trophy. Only results."

Execution means closing the loop – not just starting the process. Great sellers follow through, follow up, and finish strong. They don't rely on marketing or luck. They know when to push and when to pivot.

Traits:

- Time management
- CRM hygiene
- Clear follow-up systems
- Closing confidence

Ask yourself: If someone audited my week, would they see a plan or a scramble? The difference between good and great is often organization.

Bonus Attributes That Accelerate Success

- **Emotional Intelligence** – Reads tone, adapts to personalities
- **Tech Fluency** – Uses tools to work smarter, not harder
- **Data-Driven Thinking** – Knows what metrics actually matter
- **Peer Leadership** – Helps others, raises the bar

Real-World Pattern:

Many top reps aren't the loudest. **They're often:**

- Methodical
- Introspective
- Quietly competitive
- Brutally prepared

Workshop Activities

Activity 1: Self-Audit — Are You Selling at the Top 5% Level?

Instructions: Rate yourself (or your reps) from 1–5 in each area below. Identify your top strength and weakest link.

AREA	SCORE (1-5)	NOTES/EVIDENCE
Mindset and Ownership		
Pipeline Discipline		
Customer Knowledge		
Follow-Up and Close		

Use this to set a 30-day improvement goal with 1 measurable behavior to change.

Activity 2: Build Your Weekly Sales System

Instructions:

Design a weekly rhythm around these 5 habits:

1. Monday morning pipeline audit

2. Daily 3x3 prospect prep

3. Midweek follow-up sprint

4. Friday review of stalled deals

5. 1-hour weekly personal learning time

■ **Goal:** Turn success into structure. Consistency creates greatness.

Chapter Conclusion:
Success Isn't a Mystery — It's a Formula

There's no magic in sales. Only mastery.

Top sellers aren't superhuman. They're just relentlessly consistent. They think like owners, execute like operators, and show up like pros.

If you're leading a team, give them this model and coach to it.

If you're selling yourself, adopt it and hold yourself to it.

If you're recruiting, hire for these traits – not just résumés.

Greatness in sales is predictable – if you know what to look for and how to build it.

CHAPTER 4

HOW TO SPOT A BAD SELLER EARLY

"

Bad hires don't just miss quota — they cost you time, momentum, morale, and market share. Catch it early or pay for it later.

"

Introduction: Don't Wait Nine Months to Realize It Was a Mistake

In sales, every day a bad hire stays on the team is a day you're paying for lost revenue, missed pipeline, and potential damage to your brand and culture.

Yet sales leaders routinely say:

"Let's give them more time."

"They're still learning the product."

"They haven't really had a chance yet."

Wrong.

Time doesn't fix a mis-hire. Observation and action do.

This chapter will teach you how to spot red flags early, separate "slow starters" from "non-starters," and take decisive, professional action before you lose deals, dollars, and team confidence.

Why You Need to Know FAST

The average ramp time for a seller is 60–90 days. But signs of a misfit can appear in the **first two weeks** – if you know what to look for.

Hiring someone who interviews well but sells poorly is one of the most expensive mistakes a business can make. And unfortunately, sales is filled with "professional interviewers" who can talk a good game – and never deliver one.

The 8 Early Warning Signs of a Bad Seller

Here are the behaviors to watch within the first 30 days of hiring:

1. Blame Shows Up Early

"The leads are bad."

"I didn't get enough onboarding."

"Nobody told me that."

A bad seller looks outward when performance lags. A good one looks inward and adjusts.

Tip: During onboarding, ask:

"What will you do if deals aren't closing as fast as expected?"

The answer reveals their mindset.

2. No Initiative

They're always waiting to be told what to do. They don't book shadow sessions, ask questions, or take control of their calendar.

Red Flag: You check in and they say, *"I'm just waiting on..."*

Top performers never "wait." They *act*.

3. Activity Without Intent

Yes, they're making dials. Yes, they're booking meetings. But it's all surface-level — no learning, no refinement, no depth.

4. Doesn't Use the Tools

Bad sellers resist systems: CRMs, calendars, call trackers. They say, *"I keep it in a notebook,"* or *"I've got it all in my head."*

5. High Talk Ratio, Low Learning

They talk more than they listen. They speak in generalities (*"I usually close fast"*) and avoid specifics.

6. They Need Constant Hand-Holding

Yes, new hires need support. But there's a difference between support and dependency. A weak seller can't move without a manager.

7. They Don't Improve

Top performers get better every week. Bad sellers plateau early — or worse, regress.

- **Ask:**
  "What have you learned this week?"
  "What are you adjusting based on your last call?"

  If they can't answer with clarity, they're not learning. They're coasting.

8. Lack of Urgency

They miss calendar invites. They're late to calls. They don't follow up the same day. **Sales is a sport of urgency. If they move slow, deals die fast.**

Example: The $100,000 Mistake

Company: Mid-size B2B tech firm

- Hired rep with great résumé and strong references
- Spent 6 weeks *"getting up to speed"*
- Didn't book pipeline meetings, but blamed the product and *"market conditions"*
- Avoided the CRM. Said they were *"working deals offline"*
- Was let go after 4 months

Cost:

- $45K in salary and benefits
- $300K in missed pipeline
- One key account was lost due to delayed follow-up
- Two top reps left because *"dead weight was tolerated"*

What to Do When You See the Signs

1. Start a 30-Day Performance Plan

- Make expectations crystal clear (meetings, call volume, pipeline value)
- Weekly checkpoints. Document everything.

2. Have the Conversation Early

- *"Here's what we need. Here's where you are. Let's align on what needs to change."*
- Ask them what support they need — and if they actually want the role.

3. Set a Deadline

- If they haven't hit the bar by Day 30, make the move.
- Do it professionally, quickly, and with dignity.

"Don't coach character. Don't beg for urgency. Don't stall on action."

Workshop Activities

Activity 1: Sales Rep Ramp Scorecard

Build a 30-Day Rep Evaluation Template. Score new reps 1–5 on:

AREA	W1	W2	W3	W4	NOTES
Product Knowledge					

AREA	W1	W2	W3	W4	NOTES
CRM Usage					
Call Preparedness					
Follow-Up Discipline					
Coachability					
Activity Quality					
Deal Progression					

Discuss trends. Who is improving? Who is flatlining?

Activity 2: Post-Mortem on Past Hiring Mistakes

Have your managers or team leads review the last 2–3 failed hires:

- What were the early signs?
- What did we overlook?
- What should we change in our process?

Create a checklist of *"Never Miss Again"* behaviors.

Chapter Conclusion:
Be Slow to Hire, Fast to Act

Not every seller will work out – and that's okay. The cost isn't in hiring someone who fails. It's in **waiting too long** to act on what you already know.

"The data is in the behavior – not the hope."

Build a system to detect bad fits early. Give clear expectations. Document the path. And when it's time to move on, do so with confidence and class.

Your culture – and your revenue – will thank you.

CHAPTER 5

WHO SHOULD NEVER BE A SALES MANAGER

> *A bad seller misses quota. A bad manager breaks the system — and takes good people down with them.*

Introduction: Promotions Should Be Earned, Not Handed Out

In most companies, the biggest management mistake isn't hiring the wrong rep.

It's promoting the wrong seller.

Sales teams often make a fatal assumption:

"This rep crushed their number — they'll be a great manager."

Not so fast.

Top performers don't always make top leaders. In fact, many of the **worst managers** were once elite individual contributors. Why? Because selling and leading are **two different skill sets**.

This chapter unpacks why some people should never be put in charge of other sellers — no matter how well they perform — and how to spot leadership potential before handing over the keys to your revenue engine.

Why Great Sellers Often Make Terrible Managers

1. They Lead with Ego, Not Empathy

They assume everyone should "just do it like I did." They lack patience, coaching skills, or emotional intelligence.

2. They Can't Let Go of the Spotlight

Management isn't about doing the work — it's about enabling

others to. Poor-fit managers hog deals, override reps, and jump in when they should be stepping back.

3. They Prioritize Results Over People

Numbers matter, but the path to those numbers matters too. A bad manager will burn out reps, cause turnover, or promote toxic behavior to hit short-term goals.

7 Signs Someone Should NOT Be a Sales Manager

1. They Only Know How to Win for Themselves

They've never shown a willingness to mentor or support others. In meetings, they talk about their own wins – not team improvement.

■ **Test it:** Ask them how they've helped another rep succeed in the last 90 days. If they can't answer, that's a red flag.

2. They Don't Follow Process

Managers must lead by example. If they cut corners, skip CRM entries, or dismiss training, their team will do the same.

■ **Tip:** Never promote a rep who "delivers results but ignores rules."

3. They Lack Emotional Control

They swing between highs and lows. One bad day ruins their week. One lost deal wrecks their judgment. That emotional volatility becomes team dysfunction.

4. They Avoid Difficult Conversations

If someone can't give feedback, challenge underperformance, or hold people accountable — they are not ready to lead.

> **Example:** A promoted AE avoided coaching a struggling rep for 3 months. By the time leadership intervened, two other team members had resigned out of frustration.

5. They Crave Credit, Not Outcomes

They want their name on every win. They don't celebrate others. They compete with their team instead of lifting it.

6. They Lack Strategic Thinking

Managers must think in weeks and quarters, not just today. If they can't forecast, spot patterns, or plan ahead — they'll lead reactively, not proactively.

7. They Were Promoted Too Fast

Sometimes, leadership rushes a promotion to keep a high performer happy. But skipping the development phase creates insecure, unprepared managers who fail upward — until they crash.

Real-World Example: When the Superstar Bombed as a Manager

A software company promoted its #1 enterprise rep to a regional sales manager role. He was charismatic, closed huge deals, and knew the product cold.

But six months in:

- Rep performance tanked

- Turnover doubled

- He micromanaged every deal

- He dismissed coaching from leadership

Result?

He was quietly moved back into an IC role. The team never recovered its trust.

Who SHOULD Be a Sales Manager?

Here's what to look for before making the move:

The 5 Manager-Ready Signals

- **Already Mentoring** – They coach others without being asked.

- **System-First Thinker** – They think about playbooks, not just plays.

- **Respected by Peers** – Others go to them for help, not just celebration.

- **Can Coach Without Doing** – They elevate others, not replace them.

- **Proactive Communicator** – They manage up, down, and across effectively.

Workshop Activities

Activity 1: Manager Readiness Assessment (Self + Peer Review)

Have reps rate themselves (and be rated by peers or managers) on a 1–5 scale for:

TRAIT	SELF SCORE	PEER/MANAGER SCORE
Helps others improve		
Communicates clearly		
Handles pressure well		
Manages time effectively		
Coaches without taking over		
Shows humility		
Follows process		

Review discrepancies and discuss potential development paths.

Activity 2: Leadership Simulation Interview

Before promoting a rep to manager, conduct a live simulation:

Prompt: *"You have a rep who missed quota two months in a row. They're blaming the product. Walk me through how you'd coach them."*

Evaluate their:

- Emotional control
- Coaching mindset
- Use of data

- Problem-solving ability

- Communication approach

Only greenlight promotions after demonstrating real leadership behaviors – not based on past sales numbers.

Chapter Conclusion:
Leadership Is Earned, Not Given

"You don't owe anyone a promotion. You owe your team the best possible leader."

Promoting the wrong person isn't just a mistake – it's a system failure. The damage from a bad manager lasts longer, spreads wider, and costs more than any single rep could.

Choose managers like you choose investors:

- Can they guide?

- Can they support?

- Can they scale?

- Can they elevate others?

Selling and managing are two different games. Respect both – and staff accordingly.

CHAPTER 6

BUILDING YOUR 30-DAY PERFORMANCE PLAN

"

Clarity is not micromanagement — it's leadership. If people don't know what's expected, it's your system that's broken.

"

Introduction: Clarity Converts Potential into Performance

Sales is a results business — but results don't happen without direction.

When a seller is underperforming, or a new hire is ramping up, most leaders default to vague encouragement:

"You've got to step it up."

"We need more from you."

"Let's see where you are in a few weeks."

That's not a plan. That's a delay.

If you want a seller to improve, succeed, or self-select out, you must give them **clarity, structure, and a defined path**. That's what a 30-day performance plan provides.

This chapter teaches you how to build, deliver, and execute a performance plan that accelerates results, surfaces coachability, and protects your time — and your team.

Why a 30-Day Plan Works

A great 30-day plan accomplishes three things:

1. **Sets expectations** — No confusion about what "good" looks like

2. **Creates accountability** — Weekly checkpoints based on facts, not feelings

3. **Accelerates decision-making** — You'll know within a month if they're a keeper or a cut

"If a seller is failing silently, it's because you're managing quietly."

The 5 Elements of an Effective
30-Day Performance Plan

1. Clear Quantitative Targets

Set specific, trackable numbers:

of meetings booked

- Pipeline value added

of qualified opportunities

- Close rate or revenue threshold (if applicable)

■ Example:

"You must book 12 meetings, add $150,000 to pipeline, and close at least $20,000 in revenue this month."

2. Defined Daily & Weekly Activity Goals

Break it down so there's no guesswork:

- 40 calls/day
- 5 new prospects researched/day
- Follow-ups completed within 24 hours
- CRM updated daily

■ Tip: Don't overwhelm. Prioritize 3–5 non-negotiables and inspect them.

3. Skill-Based Development Areas

Identify what behaviors or skills need coaching:

- Objection handling
- Demo delivery
- Qualification process
- Discovery questions

■ Example:

"By end of Week 2, complete 3 mock calls with manager and receive 80%+ score."

4. Weekly Check-Ins with Documentation

Schedule recurring 1:1s – not optional

- Review progress
- Celebrate wins
- Adjust plan as needed
- Record outcomes in writing

■ Tip: Keep emotion out. Let the data guide the discussion.

5. End-of-Plan Decision Point

What happens after 30 days?

Three valid outcomes:

- Retain and remove from plan
- Extend with updated targets
- Terminate based on clear misses

■ *"Don't kick the can. Don't ghost the rep. Don't avoid the outcome."*

Real-World Example: A Plan That Turned It Around

Company: Mid-market B2B tech

Rep: Ashley, new AE, struggling in first 60 days

Problem: Low activity, low conversion, low confidence

Plan Created:

- 10 calls/day + 2 demos/week
- Complete 5 product roleplays with manager
- Use email templates with 90%+ compliance
- Track daily in CRM for weekly review

Result:
By week 4, Ashley was consistently booking meetings, had regained confidence, and closed two new deals.

Lesson: She didn't need more time. She needed structure and belief.

What to Avoid When Building a Plan

- **Vagueness** – "Be better at outreach" is not a plan
- **Overkill** – Don't turn it into a spreadsheet bootcamp
- **Silence** – Don't send the doc and disappear

- **Moving the goalposts** – Stick to what you set unless something materially changes

Workshop Activities

Activity 1: Build a 30-Day Plan Template
Use this format:

SECTION	DESCRIPTION
Quantitative Goals	(e.g., 10 meetings booked, $50k pipeline)
Daily/Weekly Activity Goals	(e.g., 30 calls/day, 5 follow-ups/day)
Skill Development Targets	(e.g., discovery, objection handling)
Support Provided	(e.g., roleplays, call reviews, email templates)
Weekly Check-In Dates	(e.g., Every Friday @ 10 AM)
Decision Point	(e.g., Retain, Extend, or Exit)

Deliverable: Have your managers draft one plan for either a struggling rep or a new hire.

Activity 2: Debrief a Past Performance Failure

Pick one rep who didn't work out. As a leadership group, answer:

- Did we give them a plan?
- Was it clear, fair, and documented?
- What signs did we miss early?
- What will we do differently next time?

Goal: Learn from failure. Improve the process.

Chapter Conclusion:
Leadership Is Measured in Clarity

A 30-day plan isn't just a performance tool — it's a leadership tool. It protects the rep from confusion. It protects you from indecision. And it protects the team from carrying someone who isn't delivering.

The best sellers will rise to clarity. The wrong ones will remove themselves.

Either way, you win.

"Hope is not a strategy. Documentation is. Put it in writing. Inspect what you expect. Decide with confidence."

CHAPTER 7

RETAINING TOP TALENT

"

Top talent doesn't leave because they're losing — they leave because they're winning in the wrong environment.

"

Introduction: It's Not the Money – It's the Mission, the Manager, and the Momentum

We fight hard to recruit A-players. We court them, train them, hand them big quotas – and then we assume they'll stick around forever if the checks keep coming.

Wrong.

Great sellers have options. Always. If your environment isn't helping them grow, they will find one that does. This chapter is about how to build a culture that retains winners, avoids preventable turnover, and gives your top performers a reason to stay – even when competitors come calling.

The Real Cost of Losing a Top Performer

When a top seller walks, you're not just losing revenue – you're losing:

- Relationships with key accounts
- Momentum in the market
- Morale across the team
- Recruiting power ("Why did they leave?")
- Time spent rebuilding

Estimated Cost: 1.5–2x their annual comp + 6 months of lost pipeline

"Replacing an A-player is harder than hiring one — because you now have to explain the gap."

Why Great Sellers Actually Leave

1. They Outgrow the Role

Top talent hates standing still. If they're not learning, expanding, or leveling up, they'll eventually bounce.

■ **Fix:** Build clear growth paths — into leadership, enterprise, or strategic roles.

2. They Don't Respect the Leadership

Nothing makes a great seller run faster than reporting to someone they don't trust, respect, or learn from.

■ **Fix:** Audit your managers. Are they coaching? Listening? Creating value?

People don't leave companies. They leave sales managers.

3. The Culture Punishes Excellence

When the worst rep gets the same treatment as the best, the best will leave. They don't want to carry dead weight.

■ **Fix:** Create a culture of merit. Celebrate and reward what matters.

4. They Feel Overworked and Undervalued

If comp is unclear, workload is overwhelming, or wins are ignored, even strong earners start looking elsewhere.

■ **Fix:** Recognize wins often, publicly. Streamline unnecessary meetings. Be transparent about comp, career path, and performance metrics.

5. You Tolerate Toxic Behavior

If toxic closers, bad attitudes, or politics are left unchecked, your top performers will check out.

■ **Fix:** Protect culture like it's a client. The wrong people push the right ones out.

6 Principles for Retaining Top Talent

1. Coach, Don't Micromanage

Top sellers hate being babysat. But they crave feedback, insights, and strategic coaching.

■ **Example:** Use deal reviews not to interrogate – but to sharpen their thinking.

2. Pay Fairly and Transparently

Money isn't everything – until it's not right. Comp plans should reward value creation, not just activity.

Tip: Offer accelerators, incentives, and clarity — no one should guess how they get paid.

3. Give Them a Voice

Top reps have insights. Invite them into product feedback, process design, and messaging refinement.

Example: Form an elite seller council that meets monthly with leadership.

4. Promote from Within (When Ready)

Let top performers grow into new roles — but don't rush it. Create stretch opportunities before titles.

Tip: Let them lead onboarding, mentor new hires, or run a training before considering a promotion.

5. Make Recognition a Ritual

Never let a great month pass without acknowledgment. Recognition doesn't need to cost money — just attention.

Ideas:
- "Closer of the Month" award
- Personal thank-you notes from execs
- Public Slack shoutouts

6. Give Them Clear Next Steps

If they can't see what's next, they'll assume there is no next.

Fix: Have quarterly growth conversations. Document goals. Build a 12-month vision for their path.

Real-World Example:
Why Maya Stayed

Maya was the #1 mid-market AE for three years. Competitors offered her higher base and better titles. She stayed because:

- Her manager reviewed every key deal with her and made her better
- She had influence over GTM strategy
- She was offered a "Head of Strategic Accounts" track with milestones
- Her wins were always seen, celebrated, and tied to company growth

She said: *"I feel like I'm still building something here — not just selling."*

That's why she stayed.

Workshop Activities

Activity 1: The Talent Risk Audit

List your top 5 sellers. For each, answer:

Name	Engagement Level (1–10)	Last Career Conversation	Risk of Leaving (Low/ Med/High)	Next Step to Retain

Goal: Identify who's at risk and what you're doing (or not doing) to retain them.

Activity 2: Exit Interview Post-Mortem

If a top performer left in the last 12 months, answer:

- What did they say publicly vs. what you've heard privately?
- What could have been done earlier?
- What signs did we miss?
- What will we do differently going forward?

Use insights to update your team retention strategy.

Chapter Conclusion:
Protect the Performers — or Prepare to Lose Them

Retaining top talent isn't about perks, ping-pong tables, or LinkedIn posts. It's about **real leadership, clear growth**, and **intentional culture.**

Great sellers are always on someone else's radar. The only question is whether your company gives them a better reason to stay than anyone else can offer.

"Don't wait until they leave to show them what they meant. Show them now — and often."

Your pipeline starts with people. Keep the best ones in the building.

CHAPTER 8

LETTING GO OF LOW PERFORMERS

> *Keeping a low performer too long isn't kindness — it's a leadership failure. Fast, fair, final exits protect the business, the team, and the person.*

Introduction: Decisiveness Is a Leadership Requirement

There's a reason many sales teams underperform – and it's not just pipeline or pricing. It's because managers wait too long to act on what they already know:

- Reps not hitting quota
- Reps not improving
- Reps not responding to coaching
- Reps who bring down the team

And yet, excuses pile up:

"I just need to give them more time."

"They're trying hard."

"Maybe it's the leads."

"Let's wait until next quarter."

No.

If you're clear, documented, and fair – it's time to move. Delaying the decision doesn't help the rep, your team, or your revenue. This chapter is your guide to making performance-based exits fast, fair, and final – with professionalism and dignity.

The Real Risks of Keeping Low Performers

Waiting too long costs more than you think:

- Lost revenue

- Declining team morale

- Lowered performance standards

- A culture of tolerance

- Your own credibility as a leader

"Everyone on your team knows who the low performer is. If you don't act, they assume you don't care."

When It's Time to Move On

You don't fire on feelings. You fire on facts.

The 4 Signs a Seller Must Go:

1. **Consistent Misses** – 2+ quarters below quota, with no sign of progress

2. **Failure to Execute the Plan** – Ignoring the 30-day plan, or failing to meet its milestones

3. **Poor Coachability** – Defensive, closed off to feedback, or blames others

4. **Negative Culture Impact** – Gossip, complaining, disengagement, or toxic behavior

■ **Bonus Sign:**
   "You've already mentally replaced them – you're just avoiding the conversation."

How to Fire Right: Fast, Fair, Final

Step 1: Be Clear from the Start

If they're not meeting expectations, tell them – directly,

with specifics.

Step 2: Document Every Step

No performance plan should be verbal only. Keep records of:

- Activity metrics
- Skill evaluations
- Missed expectations
- Coaching sessions

Step 3: Use a 30-Day Plan as a Decision Tool

Give them a shot – but with structure and visibility. At the end of the plan, make a decision. No *"let's see what happens."*

Step 4: Involve HR the Right Way

Loop in HR early – not when it's time to fire. They'll help you ensure compliance, documentation, and fairness.

Step 5: Exit with Professionalism

In the final conversation:

- Be clear and respectful
- Stay calm and focused
- Offer a clean offboarding (equipment return, severance terms, final paycheck timing)

"This is a business decision based on performance, not personal failure."

Real-World Example: The Rep You Should Have Fired Sooner

- **Company:** B2B logistics SaaS
- **Rep:** Low activity, missed quota 3 quarters in a row
- **Red flags:** Rejected coaching, skipped CRM updates, spoke negatively in team meetings
- **Leadership delay:** *"He's a nice guy and knows the space"*
- **Impact:** Team morale dropped. Two top reps left, citing culture concerns.

Action taken: After 11 months, the rep was finally exited. Within 60 days, team performance rebounded – fast.

The team didn't say, *"Why did you let him go?"*

They said, *"What took so long?"*

Workshop Activities

Activity 1: Evaluate One At-Risk Rep Using This Checklist

EVALUATION AREA	NOTES/RATING	RED FLAG?
Quota Attainment (last 2 quarters)		
Coaching Response		
Activity Discipline		
30-Day Plan Completion		
Culture/Team Impact		

If three or more red flags are present -> it's time to plan for exit.

Activity 2: Write a Performance Exit Script

Managers should write a short, direct, professional script to use when parting ways with a low performer.

Template Example:

"We've worked together over the last 60 days to improve your performance. Unfortunately, the targets have not been met and there has not been sufficient progress. Today will be your last day. We'll walk you through next steps with HR. We thank you for your efforts and wish you the best in your next opportunity."

Practice delivery in a manager workshop to build confidence and reduce anxiety.

Chapter Conclusion:
It's Not Just Who You Hire — It's Who You Keep

As a sales leader, your job is to create clarity, not comfort. Firing someone is hard — but not firing when needed is far worse.

Letting go of a low performer the right way:

- Protects your culture

- Sets a clear standard

- Resets expectations for everyone else

- Makes room for someone better

"You can't build a high-performance team by tolerating low-performance behavior."

Be fast. Be fair. Be final.

And lead with the courage your team is counting on.

CHAPTER 9

CREATING A SCALABLE HIRING FRAMEWORK

> *You don't rise to your hiring goals — you fall to your hiring system. Build one that scales, or you'll always be in recovery mode.*

Introduction: Stop Hiring on Hope

Most sales organizations hire like they sell — reactively.

Someone quits? Post a job.

Growth funding comes in? Hire five more reps next quarter.

Quarter ends soft? Time to *"level up the team."*

The problem isn't ambition. **It's lack of structure.**

Without a scalable hiring framework, you'll:

- Move too slowly
- Lower your bar under pressure
- Miss warning signs
- Burn cycles onboarding the wrong people

This chapter gives you a repeatable, high-impact hiring framework that works whether you're hiring your next rep or your next 50.

Why Most Sales Hiring Fails

- **No Scorecard:** Vague definitions of what makes a good seller
- **Unstructured Interviews:** "Tell me about yourself" conversations that prove nothing
- **Gut-Based Decisions:** Bias, ego, and optimism over data
- **Inconsistent Candidate Experience:** Hurts your brand and loses A-players

"If you wouldn't run your sales pipeline without a process, don't run your hiring pipeline without one."

The 5-Step Scalable Hiring Framework

Step 1: Define the Role Rigorously

Start with role clarity:

- What are the daily activities?
- What tools, accounts, or territories will they manage?
- What outcomes define success in 90 days? In 1 year?

■ **Tip:** Write a "Day in the Life" paragraph for each role. Don't just list vague qualities. Define what doing the job well actually looks like.

Step 2: Build a Scorecard Before You Post the Job

Your scorecard should cover:

CATEGORY	WEIGHT	CRITERIA
Sales Ability	High	Prospecting, closing, pipeline discipline
Coachability	High	Response to feedback, humility
Communication	Medium	Clarity, tone, written follow-up
Ownership Mindset	Medium	Accountability, self-direction
Culture Fit	Medium	Alignment with team values

■ **Tip:** Use this scorecard during interviews and when debriefing with the team.

Step 3: Design a Structured Interview Process

Your process should include:

- **Phone Screen (15–20 min)** – Check communication,

motivation, red flags

- **Behavioral Interview (45 min)** – Past behavior predicts future results
- **Sales Simulation (30 min)** – Live pitch, objection handling, or cold call
- **Peer Interview (30 min)** – Team fit, collaboration skills
- **Final Round (with leadership)** – Culture fit, vision, growth trajectory

"If they can't sell themselves, they won't sell your product."

Step 4: Use Simulations to Reveal the Truth

Words are cheap. Simulations reveal the truth.

Examples:
- Have them research and cold-email you as a prospect
- Run a roleplay call with a mock buyer
- Ask them to qualify your company for a product demo

What to watch for: Preparation, structure, curiosity, clarity, coachability under pressure

Step 5: Close with Speed and Precision

Top sellers have options – they won't wait three weeks for a follow-up.

Best Practices:
- Debrief with your team the same day
- Score them on your shared rubric
- Send a decision or offer within 48–72 hours
- Provide next steps with clarity

Real-World Example: How a Sales Org Doubled Revenue by Hiring Differently

A growth-stage SaaS company struggled with rep turnover and inconsistent performance. They replaced their loose, gut-driven hiring with a structured system:

- Created detailed role scorecards
- Introduced sales simulations in Round 2
- Added a "Coachability Interview" with real-time feedback
- Built a 3-tab hiring dashboard in Google Sheets to track pipeline, status, and performance post-hire

Result:

- 65% increase in quota attainment within 6 months
- 50% decrease in ramp time
- 90% of hires hit quota by Month 6

Workshop Activities

Activity 1: Build a Hiring Scorecard

Have your hiring managers create a job-specific hiring scorecard using this template:

CATEGORY	MUST HAVE (Y/N)	RATING (1-5)	NOTES
Sales Process Knowledge	Y		

CATEGORY	MUST HAVE (Y/N)	RATING (1-5)	NOTES
Objection Handling	Y		
Coachability	Y		
Communication Skills	N		
Cultural Alignment	Y		

Review your current open roles. Apply this scorecard to screen your next 3 candidates.

Activity 2: Draft a Sales Simulation

Pick one role (AE, SDR, etc.) and create a real-world challenge that tests the candidate's:

- Ability to research
- Preparation quality
- Pitch clarity
- Objection handling
- Confidence under pressure

Deliverable: Every hiring manager should walk away with 1 simulation they can begin using in interviews next week.

Chapter Conclusion:
Scale People Like You Scale Pipeline

Hiring is not a *"people problem"* — it's a process opportunity.

The companies that scale fastest and perform best aren't the ones with flashy job ads. They're the ones with a clear system for identifying, evaluating, and onboarding the right people – repeatedly.

You're not just hiring a seller. You're investing in future revenue.

"If you get the hiring right, everything else gets easier."

So build the process now. Refine it over time. And never lower the bar when the pressure's high – that's when you need it most.

CHAPTER 10

YOUR SALES BENCH

"

If you wait until you have an opening to start recruiting, you're already behind. Build a bench the way great teams do — always.

"

Introduction: Recruiting Is Not a Reaction – It's a Revenue Strategy

Most sales leaders treat hiring like emergency response.

A rep quits. A new territory opens. A promotion creates a gap.

And suddenly, it's panic mode.

But the best organizations – the ones that consistently deliver revenue – don't scramble when someone leaves. They're ready. Because they've been building a sales bench all along.

This chapter is about how to keep your sales team fully staffed, strong, and ready for anything – by treating **recruiting as a permanent muscle, not a temporary motion.**

Why You Need a Bench Before You Need a Hire

When you're under pressure to fill a seat, you make compromises:

- You rush the interview process
- You lower the hiring bar
- You overburden your top performers
- You lose momentum in the market

"A rep vacancy is more than a headcount issue – it's a revenue delay and a culture risk."

Having a bench means:

- You can promote internally without creating a hole
- You reduce ramp time
- You grow confidently, not reactively
- You never settle

The "Always Be Recruiting" (ABR) Mindset

What ABR Looks Like in Practice:

- You conduct interviews even when you're not hiring

- Your team helps identify future teammates

- You keep a short list of 5–10 "warm" candidates

- Your job description is never out of date

- You treat hiring like a pipeline – with stages, follow-ups, and nurturing

The 4-Part Sales Bench Strategy

1. Build a Candidate Pipeline Like a Deal Pipeline

Use a CRM or spreadsheet to track:

- Passive candidates you've met
- Warm intros from current team

- People who reached final interviews but weren't hired
- Rising talent from LinkedIn or networking events

Columns to include:

NAME	CURRENT ROLE	STATUS	SOURCE	NOTES	FOLLOW-UP DATE

2. Create a Rep Referral Flywheel

Great sellers know great sellers.

Tips to activate referrals:

- Offer incentives ($1,000–$2,500) for hired referrals
- Celebrate successful referrals publicly
- Ask your top reps, "Who do you admire that we should talk to?"
- Turn happy customers into future hires (esp. in B2B SaaS)

"Referrals close faster, perform better, and stay longer."

3. Turn Interviews into Brand Builders

Even when you don't hire someone, leave them with a positive impression:

- Give useful feedback
- Follow up with future opportunities
- Add them to a candidate newsletter or talent update

Why? You're not just filling a job – you're building a reputation in the market.

4. Create "Always Hiring" Signals

Make sure your public presence supports bench-building:

- Keep your Careers page updated
- Include "Always Hiring Great Sales Talent" in job listings and email signatures
- Have managers post about team wins and culture on LinkedIn
- Get your AEs to share "a day in the life" content on social

Real-World Example: The 2-Deep Model That Saved a Sales Org

A growth-stage cybersecurity company used a 2-deep hiring strategy:

- Every open role had 2 potential candidates in the queue
- Every manager was expected to meet 1 passive candidate per month
- A "bench pipeline" tracker was reviewed monthly, just like sales pipeline

Results:

- When a top rep left for family reasons, they backfilled in 5 days
- When a surprise round of funding hit, they expanded into 3 new territories within 30 days
- Rep ramp time dropped by 3 weeks due to pre-screened candidate fit

Workshop Activities

Activity 1: Build Your Bench Pipeline Tracker

Create a live spreadsheet or CRM table with the following headers:

- Name
- Role
- Strengths
- Interviewed?
- Warm / Cold
- Next Touchpoint
- Notes

Ask every sales leader to identify:

- 3 past candidates worth re-engaging
- 2 current reps who could refer someone
- 1 competitor with strong talent worth watching

Activity 2: Recruit One   Passive Candidate This Month

Pick one person in your network (or your team's) and:

- Reach out personally
- Tell them you're always building
- Ask them what would make them consider a move
- Offer a coffee chat, not a pitch

Goal: Warm up one potential future hire – no pressure, just relationship-building.

Chapter Conclusion:
Build Before You Need It

A world-class sales org doesn't just close deals — it closes talent gaps before they open.

If you want to scale with speed, consistency, and strength, stop relying on job boards and headhunters in crisis. Instead:

- Build your bench like you build pipeline
- Meet future teammates before they're needed
- Empower your team to recruit alongside you
- Keep your hiring machine running — even when fully staffed

> *"The best leaders never say, 'We're not hiring right now.'*
> *They say, 'We're always looking for the next great one.'"*

So build the bench. Protect the standard. And keep the future of your revenue team one step ahead.

PEOPLE PROBLEMS ARE REVENUE PROBLEMS

After everything you've read in this bonus section, one truth should be crystal clear:

If you don't get the people right, your revenue will never be right.

When revenue doesn't come in, the cause often falls into one of three categories:

1. **The Product Isn't Good Enough** – No repeatability, no real need, no market fit.

2. **The Market Doesn't Know You Exist** – No brand awareness, no trust, no demand.

3. **The Sellers Can't Sell** – No discipline, no execution, no closing power.

That third category? It's the one you have the most control over – immediately and consistently.

This bonus section has been all about helping you eliminate the third reason for missed revenue: bad sellers.

We've equipped you with tools to:

- Spot the difference between good and bad reps early
- Prevent leadership failure by not promoting the wrong people
- Set clear performance plans that give every rep a fair shot
- Exit low performers fast and respectfully
- Build a hiring machine that scales – not stalls
- Retain top performers so you're not always rebuilding

But let's be real:

Even with the best systems, you'll still occasionally make a bad hire.

So what do you do if someone becomes a bad seller?

You act. Quickly, professionally, and with structure.

- You give them a clear 30-day performance plan
- You coach them with feedback, not feelings
- You document progress and miss
- And if they can't meet the bar — you let them go with dignity

Because protecting your team, your time, and your revenue is the job.

Hiring is not just a task — it's a revenue strategy. Retention is not just HR's job — it's yours.

And firing is not just a last resort — it's a leadership responsibility.

"A great sales culture starts with great salespeople – chosen, developed, and managed with purpose."

You now have the blueprint. Use it. Revisit it. Share it with every manager you trust with a number. Because when you hire better, coach smarter, and lead clearly — Revenue follows. Every time.

APPENDIX
PEOPLE DRIVE REVENUE:
RECOMMENDED READING LIST

Chapter 1: The Sales Talent Formula

- **Geoff Smart & Randy Street** – *Who: The A Method for Hiring*, Ballantine Books, 2008

- **Patrick Lencioni** – *The Ideal Team Player*, Jossey-Bass, 2016

- **Mark Roberge** – *The Sales Acceleration Formula*, Wiley, 2015

Chapter 2: Jack Welch Revisited

- **Jack Welch** – *Winning*, Harper Business, 2005

- **Larry Bossidy & Ram Charan** – *Execution*, Crown Business, 2002

- **Stephen R. Covey** – *The 7 Habits of Highly Effective People*, Free Press, 1989

Chapter 3: The Anatomy of a Great Seller

- **Daniel H. Pink** – *To Sell Is Human*, Riverhead Books, 2012

- **Jeb Blount** – *Sales EQ*, Wiley, 2017

- **Matthew Dixon & Brent Adamson** – *The Challenger Sale*, Portfolio, 2011

Chapter 4: How to Spot a Bad Seller Early

- **Ben Horowitz** – *The Hard Thing About Hard Things*, Harper Business, 2014

- **Brad Smart** – *Topgrading*, Portfolio, 2005

- **Lou Adler** – *Hire With Your Head*, Wiley, 2021

Chapter 5: Who Should NEVER Be a Sales Manager

- **Kim Scott** – *Radical Candor*, St. Martin's Press, 2017

- **Marshall Goldsmith** – *What Got You Here Won't Get You There*, Hyperion, 2007

- **Julie Zhuo** – *The Making of a Manager*, Portfolio, 2019

Chapter 6: Building Your 30-Day Performance Plan

- **Michael Watkins** – *The First 90 Days*, Harvard Business Review Press, 2013

- **Brian Tracy** – *Eat That Frog!*, Berrett-Koehler, 2007

- **David Finkel** – *The Freedom Formula*, BenBella Books, 2019

Chapter 7: Retaining Top Talent

- **Daniel Coyle** – *The Culture Code*, Bantam, 2018

- **Liz Wiseman** – *Multipliers*, Harper Business, 2010

- **Beverly Kaye & Sharon Jordan-Evans** – *Love 'Em or Lose 'Em*, Berrett-Koehler, 2014

Chapter 8: Letting Go of Low Performers

- **Henry Cloud** – *Necessary Endings*, Harper Business, 2010

- **Peter Drucker** – *The Effective Executive*, Harper Business, 2006

- **Jack Welch** – *Jack: Straight from the Gut*, Warner Books, 2001

Chapter 9: Creating a Scalable Hiring Framework

- **Laszlo Bock** — *Work Rules!*, Twelve, 2015

- **Reed Hastings & Erin Meyer** — *No Rules Rules*, Penguin Press, 2020

- **Kerry Patterson et al.** — *Crucial Conversations*, McGraw-Hill, 2011

Chapter 10: Your Sales Bench

- **Adam Grant** — *Give and Take*, Penguin Books, 2013

- **Cal Newport** — *So Good They Can't Ignore You*, Business Plus, 2012

- **Angela Duckworth** — *Grit*, Scribner, 2016

About The Author

Mort Greenberg brings over 25 years of experience as a business leader, working with tech start-ups and major media companies. Rising from an Account Executive to the President of a division with 800+ employees generating $220 million in annual revenue, Mort has supported revenue efforts for various companies as they navigated the need for growth, mergers, acquisitions, and IPOs. He was instrumental in shaping the digital advertising landscape during the early days of the Internet at Excite.com and Ask Jeeves. He has also held leadership roles at IAC / InterActive-Corp, NBC Universal, Nokia, and iHeartMedia. Along the way, he launched two companies of his own, FitAd and MindFlight, and learned that start-ups are not always successful. Since 2016, he has been helping turn around distressed media properties into profitable companies for a global private equity firm. The #1 lesson he has learned in all his years is that by improving people's revenue mindset, business problems are healed, and teams are motivated through innovation that new revenue affords.

www.ingramcontent.com/pod-product-compliance
Lightning Source LLC
Chambersburg PA
CBHW061203220326
41597CB00015BA/1263